Clinical Training in Psychotherapy

About the Editors

Tom H. Peake currently directs the Clinical Psychology Internship at Eastern Virginia Medical School (Norfolk, Virginia) and is Associate Professor in the Department of Psychiatry and Behavioral Sciences. He previously directed the internship at Pine Rest Christian Hospital in Grand Rapids, Michigan while serving as Clinical Assistant Professor of Psychiatry with Michigan State University. He has published in the areas of psychotherapy research: therapy training, role induction, process variables, and applications of Piaget to therapy.

Robert P. Archer is an Associate Professor in the Department of Psychiatry and Behavioral Sciences at Eastern Virginia Medical School and an Adjunct Associate Professor in the Department of Psychology at Old Dominion University. Dr. Archer is currently on the editorial board of the *Journal of Consulting and Clinical Psychology* and has published in the areas of substance abuse, treatment evaluation, and personality assessment and research. He also serves as a practicum supervisor, committee member, and instructor in the Virginia Consortium for Professional Psychology and in the Clinical Psychology Internship program at the Eastern Virginia Medical School.

Clinical Training in Psychotherapy

Tom H. Peake and Robert P. Archer
Editors

The Haworth Press
New York

Clinical Training in Psychotherapy has also been published as *The Clinical Supervisor*, Volume 2, Number 4, Winter 1984.

The Haworth Press, Inc., 28 East 22 Street, New York, NY 10010

Library of Congress Cataloging in Publication Data
Main entry under title:

Clinical training in psychotherapy.

Published also as v. 2, no. 4 of The clinical supervisor.
Includes bibliographical references.
EDNLM: 1. Psychotherapy—education. W1 CL795R V.4 no.2 / WM 18 C641
RC336.C56 1984 616.89'14'071 84-15873
ISBN 0-86656-334-2
ISBN 0-86656-335-0 (pbk.)

For my mentors: Ken West, Prabha Khanna, Bill Albott, and Dick Houskamp; and my family: Lisa, Katie and Vicky Peake.

For Linda Rubin Archer and Elizabeth Meghan Archer.

Clinical Training in Psychotherapy

The Clinical Supervisor
Volume 2, Number 4

CONTENTS

Contributing Authors

William L. Albott, Ph.D., is Director of the Departments of Research and Education at Topeka State Hospital, Topeka, Kansas. He also holds faculty positions at the C. F. Menninger Foundation and Wichita State University.

James M. Anker, Ph.D., is currently Vice-President for Academic Affairs at the University of South Florida and a Professor in the Department of Psychology. Dr. Anker has served as Chair of the Department of Psychology at the University of South Florida and is a Clinical Diplomate of the American Board of Professional Psychology.

Charles M. Borduin, Ph.D., is Assistant Professor of Psychology at the University of Missouri—Columbia. He has authored a number of articles and chapters on family therapy and on the developmental impact of father absence.

Ronald B. Kurz, Ph.D., is Chairman of Pediatric Psychology at Children's Hospital National Medical Center, Washington, D.C. and Professor of Psychiatry and Behavioral Sciences and of Child Health and Development at George Washington University.

George H. Orvin, M.D., is a Professor of Psychiatry and Behavioral Sciences at the Medical University of South Carolina, Charleston, South Carolina, and is currently serving as Acting Chair of that department.

Glenn E. Triezenberg, MSW, ACSW, is Director of Ambulatory Care at Blodgett Memorial Medical Center in Grand Rapids, Michigan, where he formerly headed the Department of Social Services.

Merville O. Vincent, M.D., is a Fellow and Specialist in Psychiatry and Internal Medicine of the Royal College of Physicians and Surgeons, Canada, and since 1972 has been Executive Director of the Homewood Sanitarium in Guelph, Ontario. He has authored a book and over 80 articles and chapters on a variety of topics including mental health and mental illness in physicians and their families.

EDITOR'S COMMENTS

It is with great pleasure that we present this special issue of *The Clinical Supervisor* on clinical training in psychotherapy. Tom Peake and Robert Archer have done an excellent job of organizing nine original articles that offer a comprehensive view of the subject, and their "introduction" and "conclusion" provide a unifying theme. It is my belief that this special issue makes a lasting and significant contribution to the literature on psychotherapy training.

As pointed out in the "introduction," historically, this topic has been neglected, and more recent writings in this area have illustrated the complexity of such training. This volume addresses some of the issues in unraveling the complexity. I believe this set of articles will aid the educator/supervisor in approaching their complex task.

Carlton E. Munson

Introduction

Tom H. Peake
Robert P. Archer

In his 1977 article on the training of psychotherapists, Garfield remarked that as recently as 1966 " . . . . there had been essentially no research about the teaching of psychotherapy or the process of supervision" (p.68). Research on the process remains scanty with some exceptions, but writings about supervising and learning psychotherapy are increasing. The bibliographies in this book attest to that. Also recent volumes edited by Kaslow (1977), Hess (1980), and the development of *The Clinical Supervisor* offer a broadening scope in the study of psychotherapy training.

One conclusion Garfield did draw was that psychotherapy training is an ambiguous and confusing process. It has different goals, different techniques, and different values according to orientation (e.g., psychodynamic, behavioral, relational). The training is global with little attention paid to teaching basic skills. Finally, the significant objective of *patient outcome* is rarely used as a criterion for evaluating students' progress.

This climate does not strengthen the objective nature of learning psychotherapy. Rather the subjective, interactional, and artisan nature of training in psychotherapy loom as major considerations.

The adoption of one's own psychotherapy orientation is often found to be a matter of inadvertent influences. Therapists seem to adopt a philosophy and label themselves a certain way after rational weighing of alternatives, but Cummings and Lucchese (1978) report novice therapists believe and act in a manner influenced most by their teachers' and colleagues' actions and beliefs. This represents a less conscious influence. The artisan dimension of the profession suggests an apprenticeship model best forecasts how the training occurs. If it is a human process, then an understanding of human developmental tasks specific to this process will strengthen our efforts. What human processes can we anticipate as part of becoming a psychotherapist? The answer to that question, along with a consideration of relevant research and historical trends in training, is a unifying theme in this special edition of *The Clinical Supervisor.*

This issue has been divided into four main sections. The first section addresses the available research literature on psychotherapy and psychotherapy supervision. Specifically, Charles Borduin provides a review of the current literature on psychotherapy process and outcome with an identification of salient research trends and major findings. William Albott provides an overview of the literature on psychotherapy supervision including the utility of some common assumptions concerning what defines the most important issues regarding the supervision process. It is hoped the reader may take from these contributions a general understanding of the state of research on psychotherapy and psychotherapy training.

The second section is entitled, "Disciplined and Undisciplined Reflections: Views From Social Work, Psychiatry, and Psychology." We asked Glenn Triezenberg and George Orvin to provide a review of the most important issues in psychotherapy training within their fields. Their review is based upon experience in preparing mental health professionals for clinical practice as well as the authors' personal reflections. What has emerged from their efforts are thoughtful and creative reviews of the process of professional development of social workers and psychiatrists as well as identification of salient issues in training that transcend professional boundaries. Included in this section is a discussion of the professional development of the mental health clinician as viewed from the perspective of two clinical psychologists who are the editors of this edition.

The third section of this issue presents one article by Merville Vincent and a second by Peake and Archer on the potential problems and opportunities involved in developing a professional identity within the helping professions. Vincent, a Canadian psychiatrist who has specialized in treating the impaired clinician, provides an analysis of the types of maladaptive assumptions and beliefs held by physicians which create tremendous personal stress and dysfunction in their careers. Peake and Archer present a number of empirical concepts derived from the social psychology literature that are not usually linked directly to clinical practice. Status and power can be both help and hindrance to the clinician. This section describes some of the contextual issues, both personal and interpersonal, that influence therapy effectiveness.

The final section is devoted to the past, present and future of clinical training as described by two psychologists, Ronald Kurz and James Anker, both of whom have been centrally involved in the creation, administration, and certification of clinical training programs for many years. Having observed the influences and effects of clinical training programs, these experts share their impressions of the strengths and weaknesses of these efforts. While Anker tends to concentrate on the effects of training program structures on the preparation of effective clinicians, Kurz views the effects of societal and economic influences on the planning and function of the programs. Both articles provide an overview of the broader processes and structures within which the supervisory process is ultimately embedded.

We would like to express our appreciation to Tom Cash of Old Dominion University for his aid in editing this monograph. His thoughtful comments and suggestions were invaluable in organizing and improving our efforts.

This volume attempts to define the domain of psychotherapy and psychotherapy supervision three ways: as viewed in the available literature on these processes, as seen through the eyes of skilled trainers and practitioners from several mental health disciplines, and as perceived within the broad context of educational and societal influences. We hope, that in reviewing these materials, readers will be stimulated and challenged in their thinking about clinical training in mental health and their practice of therapy and therapy supervision. The volume concludes with reflections on what we have discovered.

REFERENCES

Cummings, N., & Lucchese, G. Adoption of a psychological orientation: The role of the inadvertent. *Psychotherapy: Theory, Research, and Practice,* 1978, *15,* 323-328.

Garfield, S. Research on the training of professional psychotherapists. In A. Gurman & A. Razin (Eds.), *Effective Psychotherapy.* New York: Pergamon, 1977.

Hess, A. (Ed.) *Psychotherapy supervision: Theory, research, and practice.* New York: Wiley, 1980.

Kaslow, F.W. *Supervision, consultation, and staff training in the helping professions.* San Francisco: Jossey-Bass, 1977.

RESEARCH ISSUES: PSYCHOTHERAPY AND PSYCHOTHERAPY SUPERVISION

Problems, Progress, and Prospects in Psychotherapy Outcome Research

Charles M. Borduin

Although training in psychotherapy typically emphasizes the acquisition of assessment and technical skills, it is unfortunate that so little attention is paid to the process of treatment termination. The decision that treatment goals have been met implies that the trainee and the supervisor have relatively well-defined criteria for a successful outcome on the part of the client. However, such criteria are often more implicit than explicit during weekly supervisory meetings. Frequently, it is only when the trainee (or client) raises the issue of treatment termination that criteria for outcome are openly discussed. Although the establishment of such criteria may rest entirely on subjective opinions and beliefs, the judgment about whether these criteria have been met is likely to have a profound influence upon the trainee's sense of efficacy as a therapist. Such a judgment may also determine whether or not the trainee gradually adopts the supervisor's model of therapeutic intervention as his or her own. It would seem, then, that the process of establishing an identity as a therapist is in no small way tied to the often ignored and poorly defined issue of therapeutic outcome.

The advent of psychotherapy outcome research in the 1940s was intended to aid both new and experienced clinicians in their judgments regarding the utility of different theoretical models and therapeutic techniques. More specifically, it was believed that the scientific study of treatment outcomes would provide objective guidelines to facilitate decisions about treatment choice. However, it was not until Eysenck's (1952) scathing review of the effects of psychotherapy that the issue of outcome research captured the attention of most clinicians. Eysenck purported to demonstrate that approximately two-thirds of all neurotics improve substantially within two years, regardless of whether or not treatment was provided. While Eysenck's findings and interpretations have been the subject of much criticism (e.g., Bergin & Lambert, 1978; Kiesler, 1966; Strupp, 1966), they have served as a major impetus to research activity in the area of psychotherapeutic intervention. Hundreds of published studies now comprise the psychotherapy outcome literature. Unfortunately, contrary to initial expectations, this literature has offered few firm conclusions to guide either the trainee or the professional therapist in his or her selection of a given model of therapeutic intervention.

Although psychotherapy outcome research has failed to fulfill some of its intended purposes, it has provided unexpected answers and has raised new questions that must not be ignored. This presentation considers both the present and potential contributions of outcome research to practice and training in psychotherapy. First, a brief discussion of psychotherapy outcome findings and the methods for evaluating these findings will be offered. Next, a number of salient issues which relate to the assessment of therapeutic outcome will be reviewed. In the final section, implications for research and training are considered.

SUBSTANTIVE FINDINGS OF OUTCOME STUDIES

Scientific activity in the field of psychotherapy is comprised of two complementary parts: the actual investigation of experimental hypotheses and the integration of experimental findings from completed investigations (Fiske, 1983). The latter activity has been most often accomplished through the literature review. Such reviews of extant research are intended to facilitate future research efforts by "taking stock" of what is already known (Cooper, 1979). Moreover, in theory, the literature review should enable mental health practitioners and policy makers to share in the accumulated knowledge about psychotherapy outcomes.

The summarization of empirical findings across various studies assumes that there are common research questions at issue. Traditionally, research questions about psychotherapy outcomes have taken one of two general forms. The first, "Is psychotherapy effective?," has long been of central interest to both clinicians and researchers. Recent reviewers (Bergin & Lambert, 1978; Frank, 1979; Luborsky, Singer, & Luborsky, 1975) have generally agreed that the effects of psychotherapy are more positive than initially described by Eysenck (1952). These reviewers report that the predominant forms of psychotherapy are at least somewhat more effective than no therapy, placebos, and pseudotherapies. A second general research question can be stated as follows: "Is one form of psychotherapy more effective than another form?" To date, comparative psychotherapy outcome research has yielded few significant results. Indeed, the above reviewers have concluded that no single form of psychotherapy is clearly superior in regard to long-term efficacy. Regarding short-term impact, similar conclusions have also been reached. One notable exception is the superiority of behavior therapy (Marks, 1978) in the treatment of certain neurotic syndromes (e.g., phobias, compulsions) and sexual dysfunctions.

That the above findings have been viewed as "disappointingly meager," (Frank, 1979) does not seem surprising. It hardly seems meaningful to know that all therapies are "somewhat" more effective than no therapy. Moreover, this modest claim ignores the fact that there are some very significant improvements and failures among clients who receive the various forms of psychotherapy. In a similar vein, what can be inferred from the finding that no single psychotherapeutic method is superior in the treatment of one or more of the many types of client problems? Must we conclude that psychotherapy is a unitary process, or that therapists can be viewed as interchangeable units? If such conclusions seem unreasonable, what explanations can be offered for the paucity of substantive findings in this area of research?

A number of serious questions have been raised about the methodological quality of psychotherapy outcome research (Garfield, 1978; Kasdin, 1980; O'Leary & Turkewitz, 1978; Strupp, 1978). Commonly cited methodological problems include the inadequate specification of treatment procedures, the failure to substantiate client labels and diagnoses, the use of dependent measures of unspecified reliability and validity, and the inadequate selection and description of therapists, to name but a few. Although psychotherapy researchers have begun to demonstrate increased methodological sophistication, methodological standards for outcome research are neither well-defined nor reasonably uniform. Consequently, reviewers are often forced to draw conclusions from studies of uneven methodological quality, or, as is even more often the case, to apply arbitrary methodological criteria in excluding certain studies from review.

Criticism has also been directed toward the traditional methods of reviewing the psychotherapy outcome literature. These methods have been described by critics (e.g., Glass, 1976; Smith, Glass, & Miller, 1980) as imprecise, subjective, and narrow in focus. These critics have argued that by reducing sources of reviewer bias, it is possible to extract more information from the extant research literature as well as to avoid contradictory conclusions between different reviewers (e.g., Bergin & Lambert, 1978 vs. Rachman & Wilson, 1980). One promising approach to the reduction of reviewer bias is meta-analysis. The term "meta-analysis," as first used by Glass (1976), refers to a quantitative, systematic method for the integration of a common research domain. Although a description of the various meta-analytic procedures is beyond the scope of this paper (see Rosenthal, 1983, for a review), these procedures generally apply inferential statistics and formal statistical hypothesis testing to numerically combined data from a large number of research investigations. The resulting summary statistics provide more objective criteria for drawing conclusions about research findings than do the simple narrative or tabular summaries that are commonly used by reviewers.

Aside from its advantages as a quantitative summary method, meta-analysis demands that the reviewer make explicit each step in the review process (Cook & Leviton, 1980; Fiske, 1983). Arbitrary decisions related to the selection of studies, the choice of methodological standards, and the classification of treatments are all clearly delineated and described. As a result, it should be possible for one reviewer to closely replicate another reviewer's meta-analysis and to obtain similar results and conclusions. In a similar vein, it should also be possible to identify and remediate alleged weaknesses in a given meta-analysis. This latter advantage—the potential to refine the various procedures that comprise the literature review process—holds much promise.

The recent application of meta-analytic procedures to the psychotherapy outcome literature (e.g., Shapiro & Shapiro, 1982; Smith & Glass, 1977; Smith et al., 1980) has already generated a spirited controversy. Although the specifics of this controversy are not detailed here (see Eysenck, 1978; Glass & Kleigl, 1983; Rachman & Wilson, 1980; Wilson & Rachman, 1983), it is clear that a number of the methodological issues raised by this debate could be resolved in subsequent reanalyses of the extant literature. As this procedure for debate more closely approximates the scientific ideal, it seems likely that meta-analysis will become standard practice in future reviews of the literature (Strube & Hartman, 1983).

Although improvements in the methodologies of both individual studies and the reviews of these studies are promising, these improvements alone are unlikely to make a major contribution to our knowledge about psychotherapy outcomes. The conclusions that we draw about psychotherapy outcomes are ultimately guided by the nature of the questions that are posed by researchers. When the results of outcome studies provide more questions than answers, perhaps we should pay more attention to the investigation of these new questions. Indeed, a continued lack of progress at the level of substantive findings would seem to reflect ambiguity about fundamental issues regarding psychotherapeutic outcome. While there is no uniform agreement about the questions that might be posed by psychotherapy researchers, there are a number of salient issues which might guide the formulation of cogent questions. It is to several of these issues that we turn next.

ISSUES IN THE EVALUATION OF PSYCHOTHERAPEUTIC OUTCOME

Client Variables

Reviewers (e.g., Bergin & Lambert, 1978; Frank, 1979) have suggested that the largest proportion of variation in therapy outcome is accounted for by personal characteristics and qualities of the client. Factors such as personality, motivation, and expectations of the client have all been shown to relate to therapeutic success. However, researchers have generally failed to describe how specific aspects of these global factors are related to outcome (Garfield, 1978). In the few studies where greater specificity has been achieved, replication and generalization of results have not been accomplished. One likely reason is that there are many possible criteria for defining therapeutic outcome between studies. Another explanatory factor is that there are some important differences in the goals and procedures of the many forms of psychotherapy. A first step toward achieving greater specificity in this area would be to identify relevant client characteristics (e.g., locus of control, motivation for insight) that are most often associated with certain therapeutic outcomes under selected forms of therapy. Assuming that such characteristics could be identified, it might be possible to enhance the likelihood of certain therapeutic outcomes through the differential assignment of clients to treatments.

It might also be useful to study the characteristics of those clients who terminate therapy prematurely. Clients who drop out of one form of treatment may differ on some important dimensions from those who drop out of another type of treatment. It seems likely that the personal goals of the client are a salient predictor of whether or not early termination of treatment occurs. Early identification of clients whose personal goals are incompatible with a given treatment would allow the therapist to recommend other forms of treatment that are more likely to result in positive outcomes. Obviously, there are likely to be some individuals who would be poor candidates for any therapy, just as there are persons who might be expected to benefit from most psychotherapies. Identification of the personal qualities of these individuals also would represent an important contribution to the psychotherapy literature.

It is interesting to note that researchers and reviewers alike have largely confined themselves to discussions of the *individual* characteristics of clients. Such a focus seems particularly narrow and may impede our efforts to understand why one client changes more than another. Human problems occur and are frequently maintained within a social context. Marriage, the family, the work environment, and the peer group are only some of the significant social networks that impact on the client. Although description and classification of the social relationships of clients are not easily accomplished, the salient influence of these relationships upon individual thought and behavior merits consideration in studies of psychotherapy outcome. Moreover, the growing popularity of marital and family therapy approaches also demands that we develop classificatory schemes that describe the characteristics of groups of individuals. One important step in this direction is the "Circumplex Model of Marital and Family Systems" developed by Olson, Sprenkle, and Russell (1979). This model can be used to identify 16 basic types of marital and family systems along two primary dimensions of behavior (i.e., cohesion and adaptability). In light of the demonstrated efficacy of family therapy approaches in the treatment of a wide range of apparent "individual" difficulties (Borduin, Henggeler, Hanson, & Harbin, 1982; Gurman & Kniskern, 1978a), it is imperative that we begin to identify and describe those system characteristics that are likely to enhance, or impede, a positive therapeutic outcome.

To improve the practical value of our research efforts, it is necessary for researchers to devote greater effort to the specification of client characteristics. Detailed descriptions of patient demographic and behavioral characteristics allow for more objective appraisals of treatment efficacy and generalization. Whenever possible, the use of standard measures of client characteristics in areas such as verbal facility (e.g., IQ scores), conceptual ability (e.g., Carr's conceptual complexity scale, 1970), and frame of reference (e.g., Rotter's I-E Scale, 1966) will greatly facilitate between-study comparisons. To the extent that these measures can be used by "real world" clinicians as part of their assessment procedures, the findings in this area of research are likely to have an impact on practice (Garfield, 1978). Nevertheless, it is important to recognize that client characteristics are not the sole determinants of therapeutic outcome. The personal qualities of the therapist and their interaction with those of the client also have an impact upon the various aspects of outcome in psychotherapy.

Therapist Variables

A vast amount of research attention has been devoted to the hypothesis that certain therapist variables are prepotent predictors of therapeutic outcome (see Parloff, Waskow, & Wolfe, 1978, for a comprehensive review). Although a wide range of therapist variables (e.g., personality, experience, mental health) have been selected for study, the results of most studies have offered little in the way of substantive findings. Indeed, only Rogers' (1957) three basic therapist conditions (i.e., warmth, genuineness, and empathy) have been rather consistently related to psychotherapy outcomes.

We do not wish to imply that Rogers' contributions to our understanding of the therapist's role have not been significant. To the contrary, the work of Rogers and his colleagues has stimulated substantial research in this area. Nevertheless, we should note, first, that much of the research on the therapeutic effectiveness of Rogers' three conditions has been challenged on methodological grounds (Mitchell, Bozarth, & Krauft, 1977) and, second, that there is conflicting evidence (Parloff et al., 1978) that these conditions are "necessary and sufficient" (Rogers, 1957, 1975) for effective treatment.

It seems likely that a number of therapist characteristics exert an impact upon client improvement. However, we might question the common research assumption that there is a linear relationship between these characteristics and the outcome of treatment. Can we safely assume that this relationship is not mediated by various characteristics and behaviors of the client? The answer may seem obvious, but it has been largely ignored by researchers. Therapist qualities such as empathy, warmth, and genuineness do not operate in a social vacuum. To the extent that clients differ in their responses to the qualities or characteristics of the therapist, the effects of these therapist variables cannot be viewed as consistent. Moreover, it seems probable that certain characteristics of the client (e.g., warmth) influence the qualities and behaviors that are shown by the therapist. This interaction of therapist and client variables affects the manner of treatment administration as well as the eventual outcome of therapy. The reciprocal nature of therapist-client interaction suggests that researchers might adopt a bidirectional model to more accurately describe the nature of influence within the treatment setting.

One promising line of research that at least tacitly assumes a reciprocal influence between therapist and client variables involves matching clients with therapists along some important dimensions. Inasmuch as the concept of matching per se provides no useful guidelines as to which dimensions are most likely to facilitate therapeutic changes, researchers have attempted therapist-client matching on a large number of demographic and psychometric variables. Although few consistent findings have yet to emerge in the literature, one potentially useful variable is cognitive complexity (i.e., the degree to which complexities are perceived in one's interpersonal environment). A number of studies have reported that compatibility between client and therapist in regard to their levels of cognitive complexity is positively related to improvement in psychotherapy (Carr, 1970; McLachlan, 1972, 1974; Posthuma & Carr, 1975). To the degree that these researchers show greater convergence in measurement procedures and definitions of terms, continued progress in this area seems likely.

Researchers might also profitably consider that there are some characteristics of therapists which are not easily defined, yet which might relate strongly to client improvement and therapy outcome. Interpersonal flexibility, persuasiveness (Frank, 1973), and relationship skill are all terms which seem to have eluded operationalization, yet are commonly used to describe more successful therapists. Attempts to study such qualities might first begin at the level of basic description. For example, repeated observations and interviews of exceptionally effective therapists might reveal that these therapists flexibly modify their interpersonal styles (e.g., from empathic and reflective to directive and confrontive) in response to their perceptions of a given client's needs. Such observations might lead us to redefine certain global therapist qualities (e.g., flexibility) in terms of a number of interrelated component qualities which are more easily understood and taught. It might also well be that certain aspects of therapists' healing powers and the therapist-client encounter will always defy observation and description. Nevertheless, to the extent that we can make headway in the identification of aspects of psychotherapeutic talent, we can continue to upgrade our efforts to train psychotherapists.

Therapeutic Technique

Proponents of the various schools of psychotherapy generally attribute their successes to the specific procedures that they employ (Strupp, 1982). As a result, much of the training in psychotherapy has focused on the teaching and practice of those therapeutic techniques that are believed to be most effective. However, as discussed earlier, the results of comparative psychotherapy outcome studies have been quite inconclusive. This failure to identify a clearly superior form of psychotherapeutic intervention has led some authors (e.g., Frank, 1973; Marmor, 1976; Rogers, 1975; Strupp, 1973) to question whether techniques per se contribute as much to therapy outcome as has been claimed.

Frank (1973, 1982) has suggested that therapeutic change is primarily a function of several "morale-building" components that are shared by all forms of psychotherapy. One central component is the human relationship that exists between client and therapist. Within the context of this relationship, there are a number of "nonspecific" factors (e.g., understanding, encouragement, interest, acceptance) that work to combat the sense of demoralization and helplessness experienced by most clients. Other important components of all psychotherapies include an explicit rationale, or conceptual scheme, and associated procedures which are defined as necessary for improvement. This scheme (i.e., theory) and its associated procedures (i.e., techniques) enhance the client's sense of self-efficacy by providing a plausible explanation for the client's problems as well as opportunities for resolving them. From this perspective, the primary function of technique is to strengthen the therapeutic relationship by requiring the active participation of the therapist and client, thereby mobilizing nonspecific healing factors. The specific content of a given therapeutic technique is viewed by Frank as much less important than the belief of the therapist (and client) in the potency of the technique.

Frank's hypothesis regarding the salience of nonspecific relationship factors has significant implications for psychotherapy outcome research. For example, a common research strategy for differentiating specific from nonspecific treatment factors is the inclusion of a no-treatment control group. However, the definition of a no-treatment group may include clients who receive placebos, those who are placed on a waiting list, or those who are denied treatment. Although each might be considered a proper control group, it is not clear that the same nonspecific factors are operative in each group. For instance, clients who are denied treatment are more likely to seek the assistance of natural caregivers (e.g., friends, a clergyman, family members) and to show "spontaneous remission" than are clients in other types of control groups (Eysenck, 1963, 1982). Until the time when we are more able to define how various no-treatment groups are different or similar in terms of nonspecific factors, researchers must be more cautious in drawing conclusions about what types of nonspecific factors have been ruled out.

Researchers must also take greater care to insure that therapeutic techniques are actually implemented as described. To date, there are few psychotherapy outcome studies which provide evidence that treatments were carried out as expected. Lacking this evidence, can we assume that textbook descriptions of "pure" techniques were implemented? In clinical settings, it seems apparent that therapists frequently borrow techniques which are associated with treatment orientations other than their own. If researchers cannot insure against this tendency, it will remain difficult to conclude that a given technique operates more effectively than another technique or than the nonspecific factors which are presumed to underlie all therapies. To the extent that certain therapies may be quite difficult to specify (e.g., experiential and gestalt treatments), empirical conclusions regarding their efficacy may not be possible. On the other hand, such specification and adherence to rigid technique has the potential of moving research away from the realities and complexities of actual clinical practice. Moreover, we should also consider that there may be certain limits in regard to what can be achieved through the use of any given set of technical operations, limits that are established by the interactions of therapist and client variables.

Although the contribution of nonspecific factors to psychotherapy outcome seems undeniable, demonstration of the superiority of certain technical operations with particular clients and problems remains a possibility. Proponents of behavioral methods have argued that there are already a number of well-controlled studies whose results favor the use of certain techniques with circumscribed behavioral disorders (Kazdin & Wilson, 1978; Rachman & Wilson, 1980). Several experimental approaches (e.g., single-case designs, dismantling and constructive strategies) that have emerged from the field of applied behavior analysis (Hersen & Barlow, 1976; Kazdin, 1980; McFall & Twentyman, 1973) may also hold substantial promise in the identification of salient treatment methods.

Defining Therapeutic Outcome

Another fundamental issue in the evaluation of psychotherapy outcomes is related to the selection of criteria that are used to define therapeutic change. Attempts to resolve questions about the comparative efficacy of different treatments have presupposed a consensus regarding appropriate outcome measures. However, an examination of the extant literature suggests that there is more controversy than consensus about evaluation criteria. On the surface, these controversies would appear to center on methodological disagreements concerning the source of evaluation (e.g., clinician vs. client) and the reliability and specificity of assessment techniques (e.g., behavioral inventories vs. projective tests). An underlying issue, however, is that the selection of outcome criteria is influenced by the values of researchers and clinicians. Indeed, values are inherent in views of mental health and treatment efficacy (Strupp & Hadley, 1977). Inasmuch as there are differences in values and perspectives regarding the process of psychotherapy, it may be impossible to ever reach a consensus in judging therapeutic success.

While values undoubtedly influence many aspects of the psychotherapy evaluation process, there are still useful strategies that researchers might employ to facilitate comparisons of therapy outcome and to better describe the changes that occur in clients. For example, considerable progress could be made through the increased use of multiple outcome criteria in individual investigations. These measures could be used to assess broad changes in attitudes, emotions, behavior, interpersonal relations, occupational performance, and so on. This research strategy would more adequately measure the multidimensional changes that are assumed to result from the many forms of psychotherapy (Kazdin & Wilson, 1978). Treatments that contribute to improvements in several areas of functioning might be evaluated more positively than those that do not.

It would also seem useful to assess therapeutic outcomes from multiple vantage points. Given that client, therapist, and observer ratings of psychotherapy outcome correlate only moderately (Bergin & Lambert, 1978), all of these perspectives should be carefully considered when drawing conclusions about treatment efficacy (Strupp & Hadley, 1977). In addition, the issue of consumer satisfaction should also receive attention from psychotherapy investigators (Berger, 1983; Bornstein & Rychtarik, 1983; McMahon & Forehand, 1983). The acceptability of treatment to clients may someday soon represent an important criterion by which society judges and funds mental health services. The rise in third-party payments may also demand that we provide evidence on consumer satisfaction in relation to specific forms of treatment. On the other hand, as consumer satisfaction may not be equivalent to effective treatment (Garfield, 1983; Parloff, 1983), researchers and policymakers must exercise caution in evaluating consumer data. Hence, while consumer evaluation measures represent a promising addition to the assessment process, they should not dominate our efforts at appraising treatment outcome.

Measures of psychotherapy outcome should also be designed to allow for the assessment of both positive and negative change.

Although the proportion of clients who experience negative effects during the course of psychotherapy remains a subject of debate, there is a growing literature which suggests that many forms of psychotherapy have deleterious effects upon at least a small number of clients (Gurman & Kniskern, 1978b; Lambert, Bergin, & Collins, 1977; Strupp, Hadley, & Gomes-Schwartz, 1977). Because the issue of negative effects is usually not considered in the design of outcome measures, there is a possibility that researchers have underestimated such effects. It is also conceivable that there are some therapies that are more detrimental for certain clients than are other therapies. Although the evaluation of negative effects is likely to threaten therapists and researchers alike, the issue should be recognized as one of major importance to both professionals and consumers.

Another possible step toward improving psychotherapy evaluations would be for researchers to adopt similar measures of outcome. Waskow and Parloff (1975) have described a core battery of outcome measures for potential use by investigators. Included in this battery are the Psychiatric Status Schedule (Spitzer, Endicott, & Cohen, 1967), Target Complaints (Battle, Imber, Hoehn-Saric, Stone, Nash, & Frank, 1966), the Hopkins Symptom Checklist (Derogatis, Lipman, & Covi, 1973), the MMPI (Dahlstrom, Welsh, & Dahlstrom, 1972), and either the Personal Adjustment and Role Skills Scales (Ellsworth, 1975) or the Katz Adjustment Scales (Katz & Lyerly, 1963). While the consistent use of these measures could advance our knowledge about psychotherapeutic change, the intended impact of Waskow and Parloff's publication on the field of psychotherapy research has not been achieved (Lambert, 1983). Nevertheless, it may still be premature to draw firm conclusions about the effects of their recommendations.

Finally, there are a number of other relevant outcome criteria that have been largely neglected by researchers. For example, alternatives to between-group comparisons of average patient performance could include evaluations of the importance (i.e., clinical significance) of client change, the proportion of clients who improve, or the durability of improvement (Kazdin & Wilson, 1978). Although mental health professionals have increasingly emphasized the need to promote long-term change (see Karoly & Steffen, 1980), psychotherapy outcome researchers have devoted surprisingly little effort to the conduct of treatment follow-ups or to the assessment of post-treatment factors which correlate with the maintenance of therapeutic gains. In a similar vein, the development of measures related to treatment efficiency and cost might also provide important guidelines for evaluating a given therapeutic approach. Factors such as the duration of therapy, the cost of therapy to the client, and the cost associated with professional training might all represent relevant criteria for comparing different treatments (Kazdin & Wilson, 1978). Obviously, such criteria could be used in conjunction with more traditional outcome measures and might be weighted accordingly.

TOWARD PROGRESS IN OUTCOME RESEARCH

Given that there are substantial differences among clients, therapists, and criteria for outcome, it does not seem likely that we can identify a single optimal treatment for the solution of most mental health difficulties. In retrospect, it is apparent that many psychotherapy researchers have posed relatively simplistic questions about extraordinarily complex treatment processes and human problems. Nevertheless, their efforts have not been fruitless. There has been considerable progress in the identification of cogent questions. Many authors now agree that the evaluation of therapy outcome is best guided by the question "What treatment, by whom, is most effective with this individual, with that specific problem, under which set of circumstances?" (Paul, 1967, p. 111). Whether such a question can be repeatedly answered will depend upon continued advances in methodology and classification. It seems clear that progress will be slow and that it will demand more cooperation among researchers than in the past.

Some investigators are not likely to be enthusiastic about the prospect of obtaining piecemeal answers to Paul's (1967) highly specific question. These researchers might turn their attention to the development of testable hypotheses regarding the more general mechanisms of therapeutic change. For example, research is needed to answer questions about the ways in which nonspecific treatment factors produce change. Also needed are efforts which clarify the relationships between specific outcome measures and the conceptual variables that treatments are presumed to influence. Questions about environmental and social factors that impact upon outcome and the maintenance of change also require increased attention.

Progress can also be augmented through improved communication among researchers. If researchers become more willing to employ similar assessment techniques and design strategies, the results of their different experiments might jointly contribute to our knowledge about psychotherapeutic outcomes. Greater description of the characteristics of clients, therapists, and their interaction would also enable both researchers and reviewers to continue to identify those factors that are most relevant to outcome.

Advances in outcome research might also result from increased communication between investigators and clinicians. There is a considerable gap between research and clinical practice in terms of target patients, treatment settings, and assessment procedures (Shapiro & Shapiro, 1983). Mutual benefits would undoubtedly accrue from better cooperation between researchers and practitioners. Therapists with years of clinical experience can offer researchers valuable information about innovative therapy procedures, practical treatment issues, and the perceived relevance of research questions. In turn, investigators can provide a much needed data base for the practice of psychotherapy. Other important issues, such as assessment of the level of training needed to perform certain types of clinical services, might also be addressed by researchers (Strupp, 1982).

The potential contributions of outcome research may ultimately depend on the nature of clinical training in psychotherapy. To the degree that researchers of the future are well-trained clinicians, they may be able to significantly advance our knowledge about therapeutic process and outcomes. Toward that end, supervisors might endeavor to demystify the various nonspecific treatment factors as well as make therapeutic techniques more teachable and learnable. The supervisor who helps the trainee to explicitly identify the operations of psychotherapy and the nature of his or her personal influence may directly enhance the trainee's skills as a researcher. While most therapists do not conduct empirical studies, it would also seem important to provide all trainees with at least basic knowledge in research design and methodology. Indeed, such training would better prepare clinicians to make intelligent judgments about psychotherapy evaluation findings.

The substantive findings of psychotherapy outcome studies may provide important guidelines for the training of psychotherapists. If evidence is accumulated regarding the influence of nonspecific treatment factors on psychotherapy outcome, these factors might become a primary focus in our efforts to select and train new clinicians. Training programs might encourage each trainee to adopt a treatment approach that best fits his or her personal qualities and interpersonal style. Alternatively, the demonstrated superiority of certain clinical approaches toward specific client problems might result in the development of highly specialized training programs. For example, evidence that systems therapies offer the treatment of choice for certain clinical goals and problems (Gurman & Kniskern, 1978a) may increasingly lead training institutions to provide a specialization in family therapy.

To some individuals, the continued debate about outcome issues and findings may seem unimportant. When one considers that the general purpose of psychotherapy is to both alleviate human suffering and to maximize human potential, however, the implications of this debate cannot be easily ignored. In addition, the public image of our services is affected, at least in part, by the exaggerated claims of some mental health professionals regarding the efficacy of certain therapeutic techniques. That this image has not generally been a positive one hardly needs to be stated. Perhaps even more important are the ethical issues that are raised by unsubstantiated claims about specific forms of psychotherapy. Obviously, it would seem that most therapists are not given to making such claims. It does seem critical, nevertheless, that we are all aware of the inadequacy of our data base as well as the value of continued investigation in this complex but important area of research.

REFERENCES

Battle, C. C., Imber, S. D., Hoehn-Saric, R., Stone, A. R., Nash, C., & Frank, J. D. Target complaints as criteria of improvement. *American Journal of Psychotherapy,* 1966, *20,* 184-192.

Berger, M. Toward maximizing the utility of consumer satisfaction as an outcome. In M. J. Lambert, E. R. Christensen, & S. S. DeJulio (Eds.), *The assessment of psychotherapy outcome.* New York: Wiley, 1983.

Bergin, A. E., & Lambert, M. J. The evaluation of therapeutic outcomes. In S. L. Garfield & A. E. Bergin (Eds.), *Handbook of psychotherapy and behavior change: An empirical analysis* (2nd ed.). New York: Wiley, 1978.

Borduin, C. M., Henggeler, S. W., Hanson, C. L., & Harbin, F. Treating the family of the adolescent: A review of the empirical literature. In S. W. Henggeler (Ed.), *Delinquency and adolescent psychopathology: A family-ecological systems approach.* Littleton, Mass.: Wright-PSG, 1982.

Bornstein, P. H., & Rychtarik, R. G. Consumer satisfaction in adult behavior therapy: Procedures, problems, and future perspectives. *Behavior Therapy,* 1983, *14,* 191-208.

Carr, J. E. Differentiation similarity of patient and therapist and the outcome of psychotherapy. *Journal of Abnormal Psychology,* 1970, *76,* 361-369.

Cook, T. D., & Leviton, L. C. Reviewing the literature: A comparison of traditional methods with meta-analysis. *Journal of Personality,* 1980, *48,* 449-472.

Cooper, H. M. Statistically combining independent studies: A meta-analysis of sex differences in conformity research. *Journal of Personality and Social Psychology,* 1979, *37,* 131-145.

Dahlstrom, W. G., Welsh, G. A., & Dahlstrom, L. E. *An MMPI handbook: Volume 1. Clinical applications* (Rev. ed.). Minneapolis: University of Minnesota Press, 1972.

Derogatis, L. R., Lipman, R. S., & Covi, L. SCL-90: An outpatient psychiatric rating scale (preliminary report). *Psychopharmacology Bulletin,* 1973, *9,* 13-27.

Ellsworth, R. B. Consumer feedback in measuring the effectiveness of mental health programs. In E. L. Struening & M. Guttentag (Eds.), *Handbook of evaluation research.* Beverly Hills: Sage, 1975.

Eysenck, H. J. The effects of psychotherapy: An evaluation. *Journal of Consulting Psychology,* 1952, *16,* 319-324.

Eysenck, H. J. Behavior therapy, spontaneous remission and transference in neurotics. *American Journal of Psychiatry,* 1963, *119,* 867-871.

Eysenck, H. J. An exercise in mega-silliness. *American Psychologist,* 1978, *33,* 517.

Eysenck, H. J. *Personality, genetics, and behavior.* New York: Praeger, 1982.

Fiske, D. W. The meta-analytic revolution in outcome research. *Journal of Consulting and Clinical Psychology,* 1983, *51,* 65-70.

Frank, J. D. *Persuasion and healing: A comparative study of psychotherapy.* (2nd ed.). Baltimore: Johns Hopkins University Press, 1973.

Frank, J. D. The present status of outcome studies. *Journal of Consulting and Clinical Psychology,* 1979, *47,* 310-316.

Frank, J. D. Therapeutic components shared by all psychotherapies. In J. H. Harvey & M. M. Parks (Eds.), *Psychotherapy research and behavior change* (Master lecture series; vol. 1). Washington, D. C.: American Psychological Association, 1982.

Garfield, S. L. Research on client variables in psychotherapy. In S. L. Garfield and A. E. Bergin (Eds.), *Handbook of psychotherapy and behavior change: An empirical analysis* (2nd ed.). New York: Wiley, 1978.

Garfield, S. L. Some comments on consumer satisfaction in behavior therapy. *Behavior Therapy,* 1983, *14,* 237-241.

Glass, G. V. Primary, secondary, and meta-analysis of research. *Educational Researcher,* 1976, *5,* 3-8.

Glass, G. V., & Kliegl, R. M. An apology for research integration in the study of psychotherapy. *Journal of Consulting and Clinical Psychology,* 1983, *51,* 28-41.

Gurman, A. S., & Kniskern, D. P. Research on marital and family therapy: Progress, perspective, and prospect. In S. L. Garfield & A. E. Bergin (Eds.), *Handbook of psychotherapy and behavior change: An empirical analysis* (2nd ed.). New York: Wiley, 1978. (a)

Gurman, A. S., & Kniskern, D. P. Deterioration in marital and family therapy: Empirical, clinical, and conceptual issues. *Family Process,* 1978, *17,* 3-20. (b)

Hersen, M., & Barlow, D. H. *Single-case experimental designs: Strategies for studying behavior change.* New York: Pergamon Press, 1976.

Karoly, P., & Steffen, J. J. (Eds.). *Improving the long-term effects of psychotherapy: Models of durable outcome.* New York: Gardner Press, 1980.

Katz, M. M., & Lyerly, S. B. Methods for measuring adjustment and social behavior in the community: Rationale, description, discriminative validity and scale development. *Psychological Reports,* 1963, *13,* 1503-1555.

Kazdin, A. E. *Research design in clinical psychology.* New York: Harper & Row, 1980.

Kazdin, A. E., & Wilson, G. T. Criteria for evaluating psychotherapy. *Archives of General Psychiatry,* 1978, *35,* 407-418.

Kiesler, D. J. Some myths of psychotherapy research and the search for a paradigm. *Psychological Bulletin,* 1966, *65,* 110-136.

Lambert, M. J. Introduction to assessment of psychotherapy outcome. In M. J. Lambert, E. R. Christensen, & S. S. DeJulio (Eds.), *The assessment of psychotherapy outcome.* New York: Wiley, 1983.

Lambert, M. J., Bergin, A. E., & Collins, J. L. Therapist-induced deterioration in psychotherapy. In A. S. Gurman & A. M. Razin (Eds.), *Effective psychotherapy: A handbook of research.* New York: Pergamon Press, 1977.

Luborsky, L., Singer, B., & Luborsky, L. Comparative studies of psychotherapies. *Archives of General Psychiatry,* 1975, *32,* 995-1008.

Marks, I. Behavioral psychotherapy of adult neurosis. In S. L. Garfield & A. E. Bergin (Eds.), *Handbook of psychotherapy and behavior change: An empirical analysis* (2nd ed.). New York: Wiley, 1978.

Marmor, J. Common operational factors in diverse approaches to behavior change. In A. Burton (Ed.), *What makes behavior change possible?* New York: Brunner/Mazel, 1976.

McFall, R. M., & Twentyman, C. T. Four experiments on the relative contributions of rehearsal, modeling, and coachings to assertion training. *Journal of Abnormal Psychology,* 1973, *81,* 199-218.

McLachlan, J. C. Benefit from group therapy as a function of patient-therapist match on conceptual level. *Psychotherapy: Theory, Research and Practice,* 1972, *9,* 317-323.

McLachlan, J. C. Therapy strategies, personality orientation and recovery from alcoholism. *Canadian Psychiatric Association Journal,* 1974, *19,* 25-30.

McMahon, R. J., & Forehand, R. L. Consumer satisfaction in behavioral treatment of children: Types, issues, and recommendations. *Behavior Therapy,* 1983, *14,* 209-225.

Mitchell, K. M., Bozarth, J. D., & Krauft, C. C. A reappraisal of the therapeutic effectiveness of accurate empathy, nonpossessive warmth, and genuineness. In A. S. Gurman & A. M. Razin (Eds.), *Effective psychotherapy: A handbook of research.* New York: Pergamon Press, 1977.

O'Leary, K. D., & Turkewitz, H. Methodological errors in marital and child treatment research. *Journal of Consulting and Clinical Psychology,* 1978, *46,* 747-758.

Olson, D. H., Sprenkle, D. H., & Russell, C. S. Circumplex model of marital and family systems: Cohesion and adaptability dimensions, family types, and clinical applications. *Family Process,* 1979, *18,* 3-28.

Parloff, M. B. Who will be satisfied by "consumer satisfaction" evidence? *Behavior Therapy,* 1983, *14,* 242-246.

Parloff, M. B., Waskow, I. E., & Wolfe, B. E. Research on therapist variables in relation to process and outcome. In S. L. Garfield & A. E. Bergin (Eds.), *Handbook of psychotherapy and behavior change: An empirical analysis* (2nd ed.). New York: Wiley, 1978.

Paul, G. L. Outcome research in psychotherapy. *Journal of Consulting Psychology,* 1967, *31,* 109-118.

Posthuma, A. B., & Carr, J. E. Differentiation matching in psychotherapy. *Canadian Psychological Review,* 1975, *16,* 35-43.

Rachman, S. J., & Wilson, G. T. *The effects of psychological therapy.* Oxford: Pergamon Press, 1980.

Rogers, C. R. The necessary and sufficient conditions of therapeutic personality change. *Journal of Consulting Psychology,* 1957, *21,* 95-103.

Rogers, C. R. Empathic: An appreciated way of being. *Counseling Psychologist,* 1975, *5,* 2-10.

Rosenthal, R. Assessing the statistical and social importance of the effects of psychotherapy. *Journal of Consulting and Clinical Psychology,* 1983, *51,* 4-13.

Rotter, J. B. Generalized expectancies for internal versus external control of reinforcement. *Psychological Monographs,* 1966, *80,* (1, Whole No. 609).

Shapiro, D. A., & Shapiro, D. Meta-analysis of comparative therapy outcome studies: A replication and refinement. *Psychological Bulletin,* 1982, *92,* 581-604.

Shapiro, D. A., & Shapiro, D. Comparative therapy outcome research: Methodological implications of meta-analysis. *Journal of Consulting and Clinical Psychology,* 1983, *51,* 42-53.

Smith, M. L., & Glass, G. V. Meta-analysis of psychotherapy outcome studies. *American Psychologist,* 1977, *32,* 752-760.

Smith, M. L., Glass, G. V., & Miller, T. I. *The benefits of psychotherapy.* Baltimore: Johns Hopkins University Press, 1980.

Spitzer, R. L., Endicott, J., & Cohen, G. *The psychiatric status schedule: Technique for evaluating social and role functioning and mental status.* New York: New York State Psychiatric Institute and Biometrics Research, 1967.

Strube, M. J., & Hartmann, D. P. Meta-analysis: Techniques, applications, and functions. *Journal of Consulting and Clinical Psychology,* 1983, *51,* 14-27.

Strupp, H. H. The outcome problem in psychotherapy revisited. In A. P. Goldstein & S. J. Dean (Eds.), *The investigation of psychotherapy: Commentaries and readings.* New York: Wiley, 1966.

Strupp, H. H. Toward a reformulation of the psychotherapeutic influence. *International Journal of Psychiatry,* 1973, *11,* 263-327.

Strupp, H. H. Psychotherapy research and practice: An overview. In S. L. Garfield & A. E. Bergin (Eds.), *Handbook of psychotherapy and behavior change: An empirical analysis* (2nd ed.). New York: Wiley, 1978.

Strupp, H. H. The outcome problem in psychotherapy: Contemporary perspectives. In J. H. Harvey & M. M. Parks (Eds.), *Psychotherapy research and behavior change* (Master lecture series; vol. 1). Washington, D. C.: American Psychological Association, 1982.

Strupp, H. H., & Hadley, S. W. A tripartite model of mental health and therapeutic outcomes: With special reference to negative effects in psychotherapy. *American Psychologist,* 1977, *32,* 187-196.

Strupp, H. H., Hadley, S. W., & Gomes-Schwartz, B. *Psychotherapy for better or worse: The problem of negative effects.* New York: Jason Aronson, 1977.

Waskow, I. E., & Parloff, M. B. (Eds.). *Psychotherapy change measures* (DHEW Publication No. ADM 74-120). Washington, D.C.: U.S. Government Printing Office, 1975.

Wilson, G. T., & Rachman, S. J. Meta-analysis and the evaluation of psychotherapy outcome: Limitations and liabilities. *Journal of Consulting and Clinical Psychology,* 1983, *51,* 54-64.

Supervisory Characteristics and Other Sources of Supervision Variance

William L. Albott

> Whenever you open a can of worms it always takes a larger can to put them back.
>
> —Anonymous

The literature regarding psychotherapy supervision has two salient features. First, in quantity, it is aptly described as meager (Shaefer, 1981). Second, there appears to be considerable agreement in terms of basic assumptions. Some of these basic assumptions include:

1. The focus of supervision will be on the psychotherapy conducted by the therapist (Ekstein & Wallerstein, 1958; Hess, 1980a; Langs, 1979; Wolberg, 1967);
2. Supervision involves at least two people—the supervisor and the supervisee (Ekstein & Wallerstein, 1967; Hess, 1980a; Langs, 1979; Wolberg, 1967);
3. Supervision is assumed to be essential to the learning and development of psychotherapy skills (Ekstein & Wallerstein, 1958; Shaefer, 1981; Wolberg, 1967);
4. Supervision is basically a "teaching" procedure (Goin, 1980; Shaefer, 1981; Wolberg, 1967);
5. The commonly understood goal of supervision is the learning of psychotherapy (Ekstein & Wallerstein, 1958; Fleming, 1953; Fleming & Benedict, 1966);
6. For supervision to be effective, that is for adequate learning to take place, three conditions must be met: "First, an adequate

presentation *to* the student of data in terms meaningful to him; second, the incorporation of this data *by* the student; and third, the ability to organize *his/her* experiences cognitively and to generalize from the information . . . " (Wolberg, 1967, p. 1027, italics added): and

7. Supervision takes place within an environment or setting that influences the process (Ekstein & Wallerstein, 1958; Greenberg, 1980).

The impression that emerges from these assumptions is that the practice of psychotherapy supervision should be basically well-conceptualized and reasonably systematic. The literature leads to the conclusion that variance should be small and due to such factors as style and relative emphasis. The latter factor is linked to theoretical orientation (e.g., psychodynamic). These impressions are incorrect. In contrast to a picture of supervision as it is theoretically portrayed, supervision is a practice that is " . . . not thoroughly conceptualized nor systematically conducted in most instances" (Shaefer, 1981, p. 51).

The thesis of this chapter is that the variance in the practice of supervision stems largely from a number of the differences incorrectly thought of as *just* style and theoretical emphasis. The intent of this chapter is to focus attention particularly on the role of the supervisor and the style of supervision as they affect the direction, content, and outcome of supervision. In order to do so, it is also necessary to attend to the effects of setting and supervisee. Our basic model is interactive and suggests that certain variable effects are increased or modified as a result of interaction with other variables.

THE SETTING AS A SOURCE OF VARIANCE

If the literature on supervision of psychotherapy as a whole is considered to be meager, the literature considering setting as a source of variance is virtually absent. In terms of setting, some of the variables that have been identified include: (a) university vs. applied setting such as Hospital, Mental Health Center, etc. (Dole, 1973); (b) administrative structure (Ekstein & Wallerstein, 1958); (c) type of patient available (Greenberg, 1980); (d) administrative vs. educational supervision (Smith & Harty, 1981); (e) number of supervisors available (Frijling-Schreuder, 1970); and (f) physical limitations associated with buildings, proximity to supervisors, and ancillary resources—e.g., one-way observation rooms, video-recording equipment, etc. (Berger, 1978; Goin, Kline, & Zimmerman, 1978).

Setting as a source of variance also includes such issues as whether the supervision is being offered as part of a formal training program—for example, psychiatric residency or psychology internship—or whether the supervision is part of an informal system carried out without explicit administrative sanction and approval. Other salient issues include how supervisors are obtained and assigned, the availability of procedures for either party to terminate an unsatisfactory supervisory relationship, as well as the clustering of certain personality types in different settings (Kelly & Fiske, 1951; Kelly & Goldberg, 1959).

The educational literature on the influence of physical features of the classroom on the learning process merits consideration here. Similarly, the research by Moos (1974) on treatment environment as a variable influencing behavior would suggest that supervision setting may be an important variable (Kantor, 1968).

THE SUPERVISEE AS A SOURCE OF VARIANCE

From the perspective of our interactional model, a disproportionate degree of attention has been directed toward the supervisee. A number of scholarly works are oriented to delineation of the role, function, and characteristics of the supervisee, which in turn are seen as major influences on the course, content, and outcome of the supervision process. We find listings of common problems in the technical performance of the supervisee (Wolberg, 1967) and numerous references describing contributions stemming from the supervisee's personality, neurotic dynamics, educational background, problems with authority and with authority figures, transference/countertransference, feelings of insecurity, anxiety, psychological mindedness, positive identification, identification with the patient/client, etc. (Doehrmann, 1976; Ekstein & Wallerstein, 1958; Hess, 1980a; Luborsky & Spence, 1978; Truax & Carkhuff, 1967; Wolberg, 1967). There is an unwitting tendency to blame the supervisee first if there are problems in the supervisory process. If the supervisor judges the student's gains from supervision to have been either minimal or unsatisfactory, the tendency is to look to the supervisee as the source of the failure.

In addressing deficiencies in our conceptualizing of supervision, Hess (1980b) points out that in spite of all of the attention given the supervisee, the definition of supervisee remains vague and effectively prohibits a workable specificity. His point that a supervisee may be a person with his or her very first psychotherapy case or may be a senior psychotherapist calls attention to the risk of overinclusive thinking about supervision. Are the supervisory issues associated with the neophyte and the senior-level psychotherapist the same? While there are similarities between the neophyte and the senior-level therapist, it seems obvious that many differences will be quite prominent. In our earlier stated assumptions, the informational needs of the neophyte are clearly quite different from those of an experienced therapist. In developing a plan of supervision that is goal-oriented, what is needed is a model to determine the supervisee's current level of functioning. The model should incorporate a method of assessing levels of knowledge and skill. This model must also address the issues associated with progress or development as a psychotherapist.

In this vein, two models are reported by Gaoni and Neumann (1974) and by Ralph (1980). Where Gaoni and Neumann's model focuses on the nature of the relationship between supervisee and supervisor, the model by Ralph is directed at an intrapersonal development (addressing variables seen by the supervisee as defining of the therapy process). Gaoni and Neumann's model identified four stages. The first is when the relationship is that of a teacher and pupil. Stage 2 is described as resembling apprenticeship. Stage 3 is characterized as developing the therapeutic personality of the supervisee. Stage 4 is characterized as consultation among equals.

The model proposed by Ralph (1980) presents a developmental sequence that is organized around the supervisee's orientation or choice of variables that guide therapy. The first stage is "learning the role of the psychotherapist as non-directive expert" (p. 244). The second stage is characterized by the supervisee adopting a *patient-centered* approach that is "global . . . and concretely content centered" (p. 244). Stage 3 is when the supervisee adopts a *relationship-centered* approach. The fourth stage is "the development of a *therapist-centered* approach in which there is an increasing awareness of the usefulness as well as limitations that the therapist's own feelings impose" (p. 245).

Though these models lack much needed specificity, not to mention validation, they call attention to an issue that could seriously and adversely impact the nature and outcome of supervision. Few supervisors would fail to discriminate between the needs of a supervisee who is in his or her first psychotherapy process and a supervisee who is a senior-level therapist. Not only would the supervisor be quite aware of the different needs, but in all likelihood the supervisor would behave quite differently toward these two individuals. On the other hand, how does the supervisor make much more difficult discriminations? For example, how would the supervisor distinguish, using Gaoni and Neumann's model, between the supervisee functioning at the pupil level and the supervisee functioning at the apprenticeship level? Using Ralph's model, how can the supervisor determine if a student is "patient-centered" or "relationship-centered?" Disregarding for the moment the issue of whether these models are indeed valid, the more central concern is the failure to distinguish in any reliable manner between supervisees in terms of their levels of personal development and supervisory needs.

Overall, the developmental perspective lacks specificity and clarity. In fact, most of the literature indicates in one way or another that the entire process of supervision is directed at facilitating global developmental growth. Yet we have not agreed upon course of development, nor do we have an agreed upon set of milestones that both supervisor and supervisee might use to gauge or evaluate the success of supervision. The absence of a conceptual yardstick to assess the supervisee's functioning before supervision may well preclude any agreement about the goal(s) of supervision or the nature of the supervisory relationship. Thus there may be no uniform method to assess the supervisee's progress or lack of progress. In view of Barnat's (1973) emphasis on the need for a supervision contract to reduce some of these ambiguities, the absence of this yardstick would lead inevitably to complicated contract negotiations filled with vague and amorphous terms of agreement. The absence of a clearly articulated developmental process wherein there are milestones and descriptions of the problems unique to each stage represents a serious barrier to our full realization of exactly how supervision can facilitate the development of the supervisee.

THE SUPERVISOR AS A SOURCE OF VARIANCE

In the case of the supervisor's contribution to the overall supervisory variance, there is a lack of literature paralleling that we formed for setting. Although there has been relatively little attention given to the supervisor, this is not to say that no literature or body of information exists. The works of Eckstein and Wallerstein (1958), Truax, Carkhuff and their associates (Carkhuff et al., 1968; Berenson et al., 1968; Truax & Carkhuff, 1967), Wolberg (1967), and Doehrmann (1976), do provide a body of observations and speculations regarding characteristics and issues that are more-or-less specific to the supervisor. Within this literature, as in the overall literature regarding supervision, there appears to be far more agreement than disagreement. The extent of this consensus extends to both observations as well as key assumptions. These assumptions, most often implicit, have guided the nature and direction of inquiries into the supervisor's role and have restricted the view of the supervisor as a major influence (both good and bad) on the process. Some of the assumptions which have shaped the thinking about the supervisor and the practice of supervision include:

1. Typically supervision problems are reflections of issues, characteristics, etc., manifested by the supervisee. Serving to reinforce this assumption is the acknowledged limited scope with which most student-supervisees regard psychotherapy.
2. Skill as a psychotherapist is the same skill one needs in order to be a supervisor. Implied here is that having been supervised and then having practiced for some unspecified period, one has automatically acquired supervision skills and knowledge.
3. Models and theories of psychotherapy are all that are needed to understand how supervisees learn.
4. In the course of learning psychotherapy one will typically be exposed to a number of different supervisors. When one begins to do supervision, one will model/imitate the "best" supervisor. Additional assumptions here are (a) that one has had a "best" supervisor; (b) that the imitation will reflect more than just mechanical imitation (Fleming, 1953); and (c) that nothing substantial will be lost in the imitation.
5. For the supervisor to meet his or her responsibility to provide adequate learning *in a manner meaningful to the student-supervisee* (Wolberg, 1967), only specifics (e.g., theory about psychotherapy) are needed. The issues of making it meaningful seems relegated to secondary status.

Many of these assumptions have a markedly self-protecting tone. The picture which emerges is one that minimizes potential adverse effects of the supervisor. In contrast to this rather idealized view are the experiences in supervision often shared in private conversations. These private comments about supervisory experiences often take on the qualities of horror stories. These comments come from virtually all of the professional groups, reflect many different training programs, and suggest that negative supervisory experiences are far more common than are reported in the literature. The small body of literature that verifies such negative experiences begins to suggest more precise descriptions of what these experiences have in common.

The extant literature depicting negative supervision experiences calls attention to the significant role that style plays in shaping the course, content, and outcome of supervision. Rosenblatt and Mayer (1975) used data collected from student accounts of supervision experiences and identified four recurrent objectionable supervisory styles. The first type, *Constrictive Supervision,* is described as a style that limits student autonomy to an excessive extent and employs autocratic measures such as forbidding the student to use certain technical procedures. Supervisors make decisions about the patient/client in unilateral ways, frequently without consulting the supervisee. The supervisor is well-intentioned, but smothers the supervisee. The second type is called *Amorphous Supervision* and is depicted as diametrically opposed to the first type. Here the supervisor offers too little input and direction. Supervision is seen as vague and the supervisor as uninvolved. The third type is identified as *Unsupportive Supervision.* These supervisors were characterized as cold, aloof, and even hostile toward the supervisee. This style not only failed to allay the students' anxieties and doubts but it often served to increase these feelings. The fourth style is *Therapeutic Supervision,* described by students as being the most objectionable. This approach to supervision essentially involves the students' being regarded as a patient and the supervisor's taking on the role of therapist. The focus is then placed on the student's personality without any consideration of its relevance to the psychotherapy process putatively being supervised.

Barnat (1973) also has discussed supervisory styles that students consistently evaluate negatively. The styles he identified involved issues of (a) supervisory affectations, (b) excessive technical zeal accompanied by role rigidity, and (c) supervisory experiences wherein interstaff conflicts resulted in the supervisee feeling exploited. The effect of these styles is to disrupt and seriously limit the "working alliance" (Ekstein & Wallerstein, 1958) and thus markedly limit growth in doing psychotherapy.

Cherniss and Egnatios (1977) identified five styles of supervision and had staff clinicians rate the styles for preference and commonality of occurrence. The styles identified were: (a) *didactic-consultative* (i.e., supervisor offers advice, suggestions, and interpretations concerning client and technical issues); (b) *insight-oriented* (i.e., supervisor uses questions to lead supervisees to think through and solve problems on their own); (c) *feeling-oriented* (i.e., supervisor focuses on emotional responses to clinical process); (d) *laissez faire* (i.e., supervisor leaves supervisee alone and is frequently unavailable for consultations); and (e) Authoritarian (i.e., supervisor tells in very specific terms what to do and how to do it, allowing very little autonomy).

A stylistic issue that has recently begun to receive more attention concerns the variable of *power* (see Brodsky, 1980; Gallessich, Gilbert, & Holahan, 1980; Levinson, 1980). The fact that the supervisory relationship begins with a clear imbalance of power sets the stage for a number of factors to become evident and influential in the supervision process. While an imbalance of power need not result in anything beyond role clarification (as in a teacher-student relationship), there is a growing body of literature which makes it clear that the power issue may well lead to adverse situations. In this context, power abuse that involves sexual issues is beginning to surface. Female supervisees with male supervisors seem most often the supervisory dyad wherein there are problems, although as more attention is focused on the issue, it would seem probable that dyads involving female supervisors with male supervisees and same-sex dyads will be showing some problems as well. Brodsky (1980) points out that the problems range from mild to severe, from inadequate sensitivity to certain issues to blatant disregard of the same issues. Because power and sex historically have been so closely related, some of the problems emerging in the supervision dyad reflect how slowly certain changes are infused into the various elements of our society. Certain problems, however, go beyond a cultural change hypothesis and reflect an unequivocal and unacceptable abuse of supervisory power. Sexual involvement with a supervisee serves as an example. While one may defend such behavior by noting that supervisees are adults who always have the option of refusal, this defense is blind to the power imbalance between supervisor and supervisee. Although sexual intimacy with a patient is seen as explicitly unethical, a similar abuse of power which involves a supervisee is far too often seen as a gray ethical area. Also related to power abuse, albeit frequently less obvious, are racial, ideological, and other forms of discrimination (Gardner, 1980). Supervision styles which embody such discriminations result in certain supervisees being treated differently and in ways unrelated to the real reason for supervision, namely, learning psychotherapy.

In virtually all forms of power abuse by the supervisor, the attitude conveyed is that the supervisor is unassailable. The supervisee is thereby intimidated quite effectively. The supervisee is given the message that the supervisor has a license to conduct supervision in any manner he or she feels fit and that the supervisee must adapt or face dire consequences. In both instances supervisees report that they feel they are essentially defenseless (powerless) to respond in any appropriate way.

Another style that seems to occur with some regularity is described in terms that depict the supervisor as having serious personal problems; problems that interfere with supervision. The experience of one colleague was that during supervision the supervisor seemed to be clearly psychotic about half of the time, and as soon as the supervision hour ended the supervisor pulled himself back together. She was certain that no one else was aware of this supervisor's problems because they seemed to be restricted to the supervisory sessions. She indicated that these sessions left her virtually isolated, with nowhere to turn for support. Fortunately, instances where such extreme form of personal disturbance dominates style are probably rare. Other forms, though at less extreme levels, seem to be noted quite often. The themes here indicate that countertransference issues manifested by the supervisor have effects on supervision that are clearly as influential as the supervisee's countertransference effects on therapy. The research by Doehrmann (1976) serves as an excellent reference in this regard, demonstrating not only an effect on the supervision per se but in parallel fashion on the therapy process.

A final style of supervision quite similar to that of *laissez faire* (Cherniss & Egnatios, 1977) is conducted by the supervisor with an avoidant style. Here the supervisor meets with the supervisee, but goes to exaggeratedly obvious (to the supervisee) lengths to avoid discussion of the therapy process. Discussion of sports, weather, politics, gardens, "idiot colleagues," vacations, clothing, etc. are the grist of this supervisor's mill. Pointed questions about the process or the patient are met by a vague reply that leads into topics irrelevant to therapy. Many supervisees agree that initially they viewed this as the foundation for a collaborative style, which recognized the supervisee as a colleague. It was at first comforting but became a dreaded hour as it became clear that this was all that would be offered.

Given the apparent prevalence of objectionable styles, it is tempting to conclude that indeed what is being practiced and called supervision may be diametrically opposed to what is written. Such a conclusion would misrepresent the distribution of the bad supervisory styles. On the basis of my own observation, although objectionable supervisors do exist in virtually all settings, the majority of supervisors lack distinction as either bad or exceptionally good. The average supervisor provides something that supervisees judge to be appropriate, and for the most part they are satisified with the manner in which it was provided. These average supervisors provide a much needed stability. In many instances, the gains in skill may be relatively modest but they are gains nonetheless.

Most of us can remember the one or two supervisors who stood out as exceptionally positive. A number of qualities of good supervisors emerge from the discussions I have had with psychotherapy students. In many instances the good supervisor was described as accepting, knowledgeable, supportive and flexible. The descriptions make it clear that positive supervisory relationships were centered on teaching and facilitating the capacity of the supervisee to think, and only secondarily was the focus on *what* to think. Many of the supervisors were identified as being clearly aligned with a theoretical orientation, but supervisees did not report being constrained to the supervisor's orientation. The supervisors were portrayed as accepting of their own limitations, while conveying a confidence in their ability to reason issues regarding both supervision and therapy in a productive and effective manner. They were open to input and discussion with the supervisee. "Tolerant with a sense of humor" was a phrase used by several different people to describe one good supervisor. Good supervisors were seen as comfortable with their errors and equally comfortable with those of the supervisee. They were also felt to be engaging and enthusiastic about being a supervisor and to be providing supervision at the supervisee's level. Clear in their role, they were confident that they were the ones with more information, more experience, and greater competence who did not have to "announce it." Instead they demonstrated it with quiet efficiency. These supervisors accepted that questions, problems, and errors were integral to the process and did not detract from it. Goin's (1982) reference to Winnicott's point that good supervisors are characterized as "knowing the right time to water the plant because basically the plant will grown in and of itself," seem to be implied in many descriptions.

Of course not all of the above attributes were present in each positively described supervisor. In fact, several supervisors were described in ways that deviated markedly from the positive traits and seemed to fit better into the objectionable styles. Reflecting on the conversations, a central observation is that positive evaluations seemed to reflect a mesh of interpersonal styles and supervisee needs with supervisor supplies. The fact that some objectionable styles have been present when the supervisee reports having a good experience raises a major question about the meaning of the supervisee evaluation. Is this evaluation reflective of their assessment of gain in psychotherapy skills or is it reflective of their relative comfort and discomfort with the experience, independent of gain in skill? The notion that consumers' (here supervisees') positive ratings can be viewed as synonymous with goal achievement represents a major risk in interpreting evaluative comments. It would seem imprudent to make the inferential leap and conclude that the comfort with an interpersonal experience in supervision indicates growth as a psychotherapist (Goin, 1982). It also seems imprudent to dismiss this feedback as essentially meaningless.

If the therapy process demands use of information that the supervisee lacks, few psychotherapy supervisors are surprised when the therapist-supervisee turns to ideas, concepts, and techniques that are ungrounded and often more expressive of his or her anxiety than of reasoned approach. Fundamentally, most supervisors agree that therapists, in training or in practice, have some limits to their knowledge and effectiveness and that when these limits are tested or actually exceeded, practice tends to become intuitive, unwitting, unconceptualized, or unsystematic. While this is agreed upon in principle in matters involving therapists and students, there seems to be no comparable acceptance in matters involving supervisors. If we consider how very little training most supervisors have had in supervision per se, it is relatively simple to think how easy it must be to reach the limits. When these limits are reached, what can be expected to occur in the supervisor? In keeping with Smith's (1982) point we might expect the emergence of behaviors that are largely grounded in prior experience, that is, imitation. If these imitative behaviors serve to reduce the supervisor's anxiety stemming from limitations of knowledge, then one would expect the supervisor to persist in the imitation. However, even given that imitation has effectively warded off anxiety, we should recognize that we have no assurance that the imitated supervisor was an effective supervisor. Further we have no assurance that the imitation will be of the "best" supervisor, or that the imitation represents understanding of what is being imitated (see Fleming, 1953). Alternatively, under the conditions of implicit threat, one might well begin to see the emergence of a style that is largely an over-generalization of those skills in which the supervisor feels most competent. In this latter regard, we might then expect a supervisor to turn to being just a therapist and unwittingly structure the experience so that the student ends up as patient rather than supervisee.

Under conditions of stress and threatened identity, we should expect that the psychopathology of the supervisor's personality will become operative (Grinberg, 1970). Problems involving countertransference issues should become more likely (Goin & Kline, 1976; Gottsengen & Gottsengen, 1979; Hassenfield & Sarris, 1978; Lower, 1972). Under these conditions it is reasonable to hypothesize that the supervision process will lose its orientation to outcome and begin to take on qualities of a ritual with little meaning.

IMPLICATION: A SOURCE FOR IMPROVEMENT

An important beginning is to acknowledge that supervisory tactics and techniques may become dominated by issues unrelated or inimical to the teaching and learning of psychotherapy. Recognition that supervisory style plays a crucial role, with both positive and negative effects, suggests that this variance must receive increased attention in both the literature and the practice of psychotherapy supervision. To continue to list and describe these styles is not enough. The time has come for an agonizing appraisal. We must acknowledge that there is a pervasive lack of formal preparation for supervision responsibilities. We must consider that supervision as it is practiced may be serving a master other than the increase of skills. Supervision may serve the goal of initiation and blind conformity to organizational and professional values (cf. Aronson & Mills, 1959; Ellis, Lee, & Peterson, 1978). In keeping with the idea that supervision represents an interaction between supervisor and supervisee, we must formulate better how to match supervisees and supervisors in order to maximize the probability that goals will be achieved. As we see that better models of development are needed to reflect the growth of a therapist, so also must we concern ourselves with a model of development of supervisors. In both of these models we systematically must identify the milestones, crises, and defenses, that are present at each stage (Valliant, 1977). We must refine our understanding of supervision techniques and process, and we must assign equal value to the supervisor as a role model (for positive identification with a therapist) and as a teacher. Writers such as Fleming and Benedict (1966), Eckstein and Wallerstein (1958), and Langs, Moldawsky, Linehan, Rice, Wessler, and Ellis (see Hess, 1980a) have provided us with models. However, we must expand these and incorporate data from such sources as education and industrial-organizational psychology into our supervision models and adhere less to models of psychotherapy. We must develop criteria and evaluation procedures that rely less on subjective reports of pleasure or comfort of the experience and more on whether the goals of supervision are achieved.

REFERENCES

Aronson E., & Mills, J. The effects of severity of initiation on liking for a group. *Journal of Abnormal and Social Psychology,* 1959, *59,* 177-181.

Barnat, M.R. Student reactions to supervision: Quests for a contract. *Professional Psychology,* 1973, *4,* 17-22.

Berenson, B.G., Carkhuff, R.R., & Myrus, P. The interpersonal functioning and training of college students. *Journal of Counseling Psychology,* 1966, *13,* 441-446.

Berger, M.M. *Videotape techniques in psychiatric training* (rev. ed.). New York: Brunner/Mazel, 1978.

Brodsky, A.M. Sex role issues in the supervision of therapy. In A.K. Hess (Ed.), *Psychotherapy supervision: Theory, research* and *practice.* New York: Wiley, 1980, 509-522.

Carkhuff, R.R., Knatochvil, D., & Friel, T. Effects of professional training: Communication and discrimination of facilitative conditions. *Journal of Counseling Psychology,* 1968, *15,* 68-74.

Cherniss, C., & Egnatios, E. Styles of clinical supervision in community mental health programs. *Journal of Consulting and Clinical Psychology,* 1977, *45,* 1195-1196.

Doehrmann, M. Parallel processes in supervision and psychotherapy. *Bulletin of the Menninger Clinic,* 1976, *40.*

Dole, A.A. A proposed multiple model for supervision. *Professional Psychology,* 1973, *4,* 7-16.

Ekstein, R., & Wallerstein, R. *The teaching and learning of psychotherapy.* New York: International Universities Press, 1958.

Ellis, G., Lee, G., & Peterson, L. Supervision and conformity: A cross-cultural analysis of parental socialization values. *American Journal of Sociology,* 1978, *84,* 386-403.

Fleming, J. The role of supervision in psychiatric training. *Bulletin of the Menninger Clinic,* 1953, *17,* 157-169.

Fleming, J. Teaching the basic skills of psychotherapy. *Archives of General Psychiatry,* 1967, *16,* 416-426.
Fleming, J., & Benedict, T. *Psychoanalytic supervision.* New York: Grune & Stratton, 1966.
Frijling-Schreuder, E.C.M. On individual supervision. *International Journal of Psycho-Analysis,* 1970, *51,* 363-370.
Gallessich, J., Gilbert, L.A., & Holahan, C.K. A training model to facilitate professional effectiveness in power- and sex- salient situations. *Professional Psychology,* 1980, *11,* 15-23.
Gaoni, B., & Neumann, M. Supervision from the point of view of the supervisee. *American Journal of Psychotherapy,* 1974, *23,* 108-114.
Gardner, L.M.H. Racial, ethnic, and social class considerations in psychotherapy supervision. In A.K. Hess (Ed.), *Psychotherapy supervision: Theory, research and practice.* New York: Wiley, 1980, 474-508.
Goin, M. Basic principles of psychotherapy supervision. In *The art of psychotherapy: Highlights of the third annual Vail Conference of the Menninger Foundation.* Philadelphia: Smithkline, 1982, 1-8.
Goin, M., & Kline, F. Countertransference: A neglected subject in supervision. *American Journal of Psychotherapy,* 1976, *133,* 41-44.
Goin, M., Kline, F., & Zimmerman, W. The use of videotapes in teaching supervision. *Journal of Psychiatric Education,* 1978, *2,* 189-196.
Gottsegen, G.B., & Gottsegen, M.G. Countertransference—the professional identity defense. *Psychotherapy: Theory, Research and Practice,* 1979, *16,* 57-60.
Greenberg, L. Supervision from the perspective of the supervisee. In A.K. Hess (Ed.), *Psychotherapy supervision: Theory, research, and practice.* New York: Wiley, 1980, 85-91.
Grinberg, L. The problems of supervision in psychoanalytic education. *International Journal of Psycho-Analysis,* 1970, *51,* 371-383.
Hassenfeld, I.N., & Sarris, J.G. Hazards and horizons of psychotherapy supervision. *American Journal of Psychotherapy,* 1978, *32,* 393-401.
Hess, A.K. (Ed.) *Psychotherapy supervision: Theory, research, and practice.* New York: Wiley, 1980(a).
Hess, A.K. Summing up and moving forward in psychotherapy supervision. In A.K. Hess (Ed.), *Psychotherapy supervision: Theory, research, and practice.* New York: Wiley, 1980(b), 525-530.
Kantor, J.R. Behaviorism in the history of psychotherapy. *The Psychological Record,* 1968, *18,* 151-166.
Kelly, E.L., & Fiske, D.W. *The prediction of performance in clinical psychology.* Ann Arbor: University of Michigan Press, 1951.
Kelly, E.L., & Goldberg, L.R. Correlates of later performance and specialization in psychotherapy, a follow-up study of trainees assessed in the VA Selection Research Project. *Psychological Monographs,* 1959, *73* (Whole No. 482).
Kriedt, P.H. Vocational interests of psychologists. *Journal of Applied Psychology,* 1949, *33,* 482-488.
Langs, R. *The supervisory experience.* New York: Jason Aronson, 1979.
Levinson, H. Power, leadership, and the management of stress. *Professional Psychology,* 1980, *11,* 497-508.
Lower, R.B. Countertransference resistances in the supervisory situation. *American Journal of Psychiatry,* 1972, *129,* 156-160.
Luborsky, L., & Spence, D.R. Quantitative research on psychoanalytic therapy. In S.L. Garfield & A.E. Bergin (Eds.), *Handbook of psychotherapy and behavior change: An empirical analysis* (2nd Ed.). New York: Wiley, 1978, 331-368.
Moos, R.H. *Evaluating treatment environments.* New York: Wiley-Interscience, 1974.
Ralph, N.B. Learning psychotherapy: A developmental perspective. *Psychiatry,* 1980, *43,* 243-250.

Rosenblatt, A., & Mayer, J.E. Objectionable supervisory styles: Student's views. *Social Work,* 1975, 184-189.

Sheafer, A.B. Clinical supervision. In C.E. Walker (Ed.), *Clinical practice of psychology.* Elmsford, N.Y.: Pergamon, 1981, 50-61.

Smith, W.H. Evaluation of the supervisory process. In *The art of psychotherapy: Highlights of the third annual Vail Conference of the Menninger Foundation.* Philadelphia: Smithkline, 1982, 9-14.

Smith, W.H., & Harty, M.D. Issues in the supervision of diagnostic testing. *Bulletin of the Menninger Clinic,* 1981, *45,* 55-61.

Solnit, A.J. Learning from psychoanalytic supervision. *International Journal of Psycho-Analysis,* 1970, *51,* 359-362.

Tophoff, M. Psychotherapy and the paradox of expertise. *Psychotherapy: Theory, Research and Practice,* 1976, *13,* 316-320.

Truax, C., & Carkhuff, R.R. *Toward effective counseling and psychotherapy: Training and practice.* Chicago: Aldine, 1967.

Valliant, G. *Adaptation to life.* Boston: Little, Brown and Company, 1977.

Wolberg, L. *The techniques of psychotherapy: Vol. 2* (2nd Ed.). New York: Grune & Stratton, 1967, 1027-1054.

DISCIPLINED AND UNDISCIPLINED REFLECTIONS: VIEWS FROM SOCIAL WORK, PSYCHIATRY, AND PSYCHOLOGY

Learning Magic: Social Work Internship and Beyond

Glenn E. Triezenberg

Clinical social workers, the least prestigious but most prodigious members of the fraternity of mental health professionals, struggle with the process of teaching and learning the skills and art of their trade. A variety of efficient and effective, as well as foolish and convoluted, methods are used in training the social work clinician.

The educational process of graduate social work education for clinically-oriented students is based on both academics and practice internship. Concentrated academic course work in human development and behavior, and a strong emphasis on research methods and theories, gives most social work graduate students the background for extensive supervised clinical experience in their internship settings. Graduate social work education and internship practice are demanding for both the student intern and the supervisor. Serious graduate schools make serious demands on students and supervisors alike. Supervisors leave lasting impressions, positive and otherwise, on the student intern.

The process of supervising clinically-oriented students is the primary domain of the graduate intern supervisor. He or she must assess the clinical acumen and knowledge base of the student while carefully reviewing the intern's practice strengths, weaknesses, and vulnerabilities. The supervisor must also assess major gaps in the intern's practice knowledge and fill these gaps in the process of supervision. Many supervisors focus the supervisory process exclusively on knowledge-building and practice-gap filling. Others more appropriately and more realistically begin the supervisory task by coaching and encouraging the intern to use the knowledge he or she already has while learning as much from the supervisor as possible.

In the context of the intern's specific assignment and the clinical supervisor's skills, the relationship and learning process take on a unique character and quality. Clinical social work supervisors generally accept interns for supervision because the supervisors enjoy teaching. Many supervisors genuinely feel that they have a contribution to offer the student and the profession. Supervisors also rely on their own past learning experiences, including clinical internships, to teach students under their supervision. Supervisory social work techniques vary extensively; however, many supervisors rely on some type of problem-identification and problem-solving approach as the basis for their teaching and intern supervision.

Understanding human behavior, healthy and pathological, in the context of specific environments, and attempting to change that behavior where appropriate and desirable, are the challenges confronting the social work intern and supervisor. Student social work interns and supervising social workers tend to use approaches to diagnosis and treatment that are conceptually elegant and simple. The terms *elegant* and *simple* are complementary, not contradictory. It is important to note that while these problem-identification/problem-solving teaching and practice approaches may be conceptually simple at the theoretical level, they are profoundly difficult to master at the practice level. What mental health practitioner, social worker, psychologist, or psychiatrist, confronted with an acting out, symptomatic, conflictual, and chaotic family situation, has not marveled at the straightforward family system intervention concepts and strategies of Virginia Satir? Satir's conceptual and practice approach is simple, elegant, and effective.

Murray Bowen, a pioneer family therapist and theorist, has called the experience of family therapy a "benevolent ordeal." A benevolent ordeal also aptly characterizes the supervisory relationships.

Under less than ideal circumstances, the supervisory relationship, or ordeal, between intern and supervisor may be considered less than benevolent. In fact, some supervisory relationships become uniquely miserable ordeals. Obviously, the quality of the supervisory relationship depends on many variables, not the least of which are the performance expectations and relationships chemistries carried into the supervisory relationship by the participants. Internship supervisors clearly have the upper hand in structuring and controlling the nature of the supervision. They decide where to place the hurdles and how high to set them. The supervisor decides the *pacing* and *clearance* factors that the student intern must satisfy.

Supervisors are "medicine men" holding magic. Credentials and practice skills are the magic supervisors possess and the interns want. Getting some magic of your own involves jumping supervisory hurdles at the prescribed height and pace. Getting some magic of your own means that the intern must involve himself or herself in some level of gamesmanship or persuasive lobbying of the sort he or she perhaps never dreamed of. Of course in the training, or supervisory environment, gamesmanship and the art of persuasion are never identified in such clear terms. Suffice it to say that students who want "the magic" must assume the appropriate learning style chosen by their supervisor. This learning style generally approximates the supervisor's diagnostic categorization of the intern's personality.

The following categories are commonly used by supervisors to characterize intern personality in learning style or orientation: (a) passive-reflective (b) passive-aggressive, (c) passive-resistive, (d) not passive and in need of therapy. A few descriptive comments about these characterizations are in order. Supervisors and interns will no doubt find these examples all-inclusive and comprehensive.

THE PASSIVE-REFLECTIVE INTERN

Passive-reflective interns are a small and somewhat select group. They are, however, composed of the most physically and intellectually gifted students. Ugly interns or interns of less than gifted intellectual prowess need not apply.

The typical passive-reflective intern hangs on the supervisor's every word and anticipates the supervisor's every request. Excellent listening skills such as these, as well as consistent demonstration of profound empathy in communicating with the supervisor, are well-rewarded at evaluation time. Passive-reflective students find the supervisory experience stimulating and rewarding. Many of them parlay their considerable intuitive and persuasive talents into future successful private practice. Some later specialize in treating the psychopathologies of the rich and famous.

THE PASSIVE-AGGRESSIVE INTERN

The passive-aggressive interns frustrate supervisors because they are bright enough to be passive, but not bright enough to permit the supervisor to be in absolute control of the relationship at all times. Trust is a significant problem in these relationships and it is usually lacking or totally absent in the relationship. A few passive-aggressive students have been known to survive the ordeal of their training. Some have later reported that the process of supervision taught them new behind-the-scenes maneuvering techniques. These often proved useful as passive-aggressive interns became clinical supervisors themselves.

THE PASSIVE-RESISTIVE INTERN

Passive-resistive social workers are the most common of the four supervisory typologies. They test supervisory authority and battle supervisors for control. Given the power vested in a supervisor, the compromises struck to balance the relationship and control the resistive intern almost always produce a more reflective and appreciative intern by year end.

THE "NOT PASSIVE, IN-NEED-OF-THERAPY INTERN"

The not-passive and in-need-of-therapy intern group, also called "actor-outers," pay dearly for their precocious attitudes and nondeferring style. It can be predicted with 100% certainty that the not-passive and in-need-of-therapy intern will become the unwitting recipient of twice-weekly supervisory psychotherapy. Interns in this classification group rarely have any choice in the matter of their supervision. Their supervision or imposed psychotherapy becomes the price paid for future credentials and inheritance of magic. Actor-outer interns enduring supervisory psychotherapy are occasionally given strange homework assignments designed to change their behavior. Imagine being told in supervisory psychotherapy by your supervisor to "Go home and think about your thinking." Also imagine asking for supervisory advice regarding how to best respond to a suicidal client who has just informed you over the phone that he is about to commit suicide by jumping off a bridge. In such a case how does the following supervisory response measure up? "Don't worry about it. Callers don't jump—jumpers don't call." An intern subjected to a full year of unrelenting supervisory psychotherapy in which he or she is given assignments like "Think about your thinking" or advice like "Callers don't jump—jumpers don't call," may question the price being paid for credentials and magic.

PREDICTABLE PRACTICE CRISES

Gail Sheehy (1981), in her book *Pathfinders,* traces the developmental life course of mature adults who successfully negotiate the numerous crises and tragedies of adulthood. Pathfinders, according to Sheehy, are not paragons of success or people who missed the tragedies of life. They are simply people who seek "uncommon solutions to common life crises." When social work interns graduate and are given the magic and the credentials to practice their trade, they become pathfinders of a sort. Career choices, practice preferences, and choices regarding area of specialization beckon and force decisions on these new professionals.

At some point these newly-graduated clinicians come to grips with two predictable practice crises. These are: (a) what I learned in graduate school doesn't work in actual practice; and, (b) the graduate school and internship did not teach me enough or prepare me adequately for real world practice.

These first predictable crisis issues separate the serious clinicians from the role players. It has been frequently observed that serious, conscientious social work clinicians, when faced with the above-noted crises, look for and get involved in meaningful supervision. Graduate school and internship prepared them to cope with the tip of the practice iceberg and taught them some clinical reasoning and conceptual thinking. This training fortunately included some awareness and knowledge regarding knowing when help is needed.

New social work clinicians may choose to resolve their initial practice anxiety and sense of being overwhelmed by involving themselves in specialty training or post-graduate supervisory programs. These supervisory support mechanisms give the therapist a sense of professional identity and a new source of supervisory support.

Training programs that focus on special forms of psychotherapy (e.g., ego psychology, Gestalt psychology, group psychotherapy, marital and family therapy, etc.) resolve the threats in early practice competency to a degree, and they ease the intern's transition into real world psychopathology and psychotherapy. Training programs of this type also provide the new clinicians with an opportunity to formulate and develop distinctive competencies.

Developing a distinctive practice competency is strategically important, if not imperative, for new social work clinicians. The world is full of therapists; therefore, it is vital to be special, to have a distinctive competence that translates into a competitive advantage. The social worker who wants to be a pathfinder must find and develop a competitive edge.

Clinically trained social workers who desire long careers in their chosen specialties often find that interest and commitment to these goals are difficult to sustain. Despite the fact that clinical social workers do more psychotherapy than psychologists and psychiatrists combined, and despite the fact that the quality and outcome level of this psychotherapy is roughly equivalent to that provided by psychology and psychiatry, it is interesting to note that the career status and salary ranges for social work are significantly lower than those offered for similar practice in psychology and psychiatry. Some social workers argue that this inequity and injustice qualifies the profession for "victim status." Our society and culture have given victim status to women and minorities because throughout history, they have experienced oppression and discrimination. Provisions of equal pay for equal work have been regularly and systematically denied to minorities and women. It would follow, therefore, that bona fide victim status could be argued for the social work profession, especially those clinical social workers of the profession who are commonly overworked and underpaid as compared to other mental health professionals doing the same or similar work.

Given the inequities of status and salary experienced by many clinical social workers, it is not surprising to find that many clinicians do not stay in the profession. They leave clinical work in search of other challenges and opportunities that offer more financial and personal payoff. Some social workers, frustrated by the limitations of clinical practice, find opportunities in administrative or management roles. It is not uncommon for graduate social work clinicians to become program managers or directors, often within five years of graduation. The clinical and interpersonal skills developed during internship and early practice years can become valuable and marketable assets. Professional social work managers, with problem-solving people skills, not to mention the credentials and magic learned from internship, are valuable commodities and resources for non-profit and industrial employers.

The transition from clinical social work to other vocational arenas (such as management, academia, or consulting) triggers a guilt crisis of sorts. Social workers making career changes of these types begin to seek the esteem and status offered by the new opportunity while at the same time feeling some loss and grief. Finding a niche that is consistent with one's professional training and growth ambitions, however one defines these entities, is fundamentally the result of serious self-analysis and action planning. The aware professional, no matter which particular discipline, must be aware of his or her specific talents and distinctive competencies in the context of environmental opportunities. Planning, decision-making, commitment-making, and the follow-through are all vitally important in self-analysis and opportunity-making. Social workers and others who would be pathfinders are reminded by Gail Sheehy to seek "uncommon solutions to common problems." We are all, as John Gardner reminds us, "continually faced with great opportunities brilliantly disguised as insoluble problems."

Maslow's (1954) theory of motivation applied to social work training and career progression choices offer some general insights into why social workers may choose the profession, and once there, why they pursue specific goals and options. Maslow's theory of motivation is based on the following premises:

1. A person will have many needs.
2. These needs may vary in importance and therefore can be ranked in a hierarchy.

3. The person will seek to satisfy the most important needs first.
4. When the person succeeds in satisfying an important need, it will cease being a motivation for the time being.
5. The person will then turn his or her attention to the next most important need.

SOCIAL WORK PRACTICE AND BEYOND

Maslow's premises make the practice behavior and career choices of professional social workers and others somewhat more understandable. During internship, survival and safety factors motivate the intern's behavior. Although physical threats from supervisors are rare, psychological well-being and success goals cannot be taken for granted. Interns in training have a need to belong, a need to be accepted. Supervisory approval and praise is vitally important and fervently sought after. After the fight-flight themes of supervision are resolved, some degree of acceptance and intimacy is often achieved in terms of professional belongingness and kinship. Then new goals emerge. These new goals tend to be somewhat more narcissistic and competitive as one's professional life develops. Although supervisory threats disappear after professional credentialing occurs, self-esteem and status emerge as replacement motivators through the first few years of professional practice.

In the first third of one's career development, making the grade and developing a professional identity are paramount needs and goals. In the second or middle third of one's professional career, the primary motivators seem to focus more on the perceived need for high professional standing and/or high perceived competence. Mid-career clinicians pay great homage to the gods of mastery, reputation, and prestige. Then suddenly an abrupt change occurs. The need for recognition, and recognition as a motivator, lose their significance. By some mysterious process the pursuit of fame, glory, and prestige seems unimportant and rather insignificant. And in the words of that famous cowboy Roy Rogers, "It don't matter" anymore.

Mid-career social work clinicians who have passed through the milestone adaptive and developmental stages of professional identity formation and career establishment ultimately must come to terms with themselves—with personal values and self-realization themes. High professional identity offers little lasting satisfaction in and of itself. Unfortunately this becomes clear only after it has been purchased at great cost. The distinctive competencies and prestige associated with high professional identity add status and esteem to the enjoyment of life, but they do not ultimately offer satisfaction.

Becoming personally and professionally self-actualized means coming to grips with self, and working and learning to love and appreciate yourself, your values, and your niche in life. It seems that what is personally and professionally satisfying in the most important analysis is the process of coming to terms with one's own unique, personal, professional, pompous, and paltry *self.*

REFERENCES

Maslow, A.H. *Motivation and personality.* New York: Harper and Row, 1954.
Rogers, Roy. Personal Communication.
Sheehy, G. *Pathfinders.* New York: Bantam Books, 1981.

The Education, Training, and Development of the Psychiatrist

George H. Orvin

A residency training program in psychiatry must have two major objectives in its structure. As with most training programs there must be available a large body of information regarding the disordered mental and emotional functioning of the human being. This information must be acquired by the resident and integrated into an extensive understanding of the normal psychologic functioning of the individual as well as the pathologic dysfunction. If a residency training program succeeds in this its first objective, it is nonetheless a failure if it does not succeed in its second. At the end of four years a resident should have acquired a large body of information that describes the normal emotional and mental health of one's fellow humans and the pathologic states which might afflict them. However, those four years must accomplish more than the acquisition of knowledge; they must bring about a change in the way the resident thinks, feels, and conducts his or her life.

The process of education for the trainee in psychiatry, as in other fields of mental health, is energized by the conduct of supervision. There should occur a gradual evolution of the professional as he or she moves toward an understanding of the field and an understanding of self. The accumulation of facts and theoretical concepts do much to provide a basis of confidence which, in turn, allows the trainee to approach the professional task with less anxiety. In other fields of medicine the acquisition of knowledge represents a much greater attainment than the development of knowledge of self. In all fields of medicine, development of judgment and wisdom are crucial to the full blossom of the professional identity but in psychiatry something more is needed. The end-product of the residency training program must be at least the initiation of the development of self-awareness, self-understanding, and an approach to self-satisfaction. Supervision of the resident in psychiatry oversees the acquisition of knowledge and skills, monitors the evolution of competence and confidence, seeks evidence of personal growth of the resident, and validates success of the supervisory process. The preparation of the psychiatrist succeeds or fails depending upon the quality of supervision. Candidates for residency training should evaluate prospective programs based on several considerations not the least of which is the quality of the supervision available to residents. Since the process of psychiatric supervision is generally not understood by the medical student, it is not surprising if he or she fails to make adequate inquiry about it in selection of a residency. However, good psychiatric training programs do not become good programs without good supervision. The candidate for psychiatric residency training faces a wide variety of programs in the selection process. Philosophical considerations might be a major influence in the decision-making process insofar as a program can be clearly identified as expressing a well-delineated treatment philosophy. The candidate should have some idea as to what his or her interests are, but since it is difficult to know in advance how one's interests will develop, it is wise to avoid overemphasis on a particular school of thought. Instead, one should seek a program with diversity of thought but singularity of purpose in the pursuit of good supervision.

Supervision is the coin of the realm in the marketplace of psychiatric residency training. It is the medium of exchange between the resident and the training program and becomes the valued compensation earned by the resident for the services rendered to the institution that educates the resident. Although the trainee receives a salary for his or her services, few would consider it as sufficient to attract and maintain a physician without additional benefits. Most resident candidates would be suspicious of training programs that offer only money for services rendered. Supervision is the keystone of all resident education in that it provides a monitoring of the trainee's acquisition of knowledge. For the psychiatric resident, supervision affords more than a scrutiny of the trainee's work; it becomes the process by which he or she comes to understand not only the patients but also the self. It initiates and perpetuates a searching of and transactions with oneself, one's environment, and one's fellow human beings. The searching begins in the interactions between the resident and his or her supervisor. Within the process of supervision are delineated the blind spots of unawareness which sponsor and support maladaptive attitudes and behaviors brought to the training experience by all who come.

Without the process of supervision the resident would learn about the patient's behaviors but little about why the patient must do some of the things which ultimately bring pain and unhappiness. Furthermore, without the process of supervision, the resident would learn little of himself or herself and consequently know little of the compassionate kinship necessary for the understanding of the suffering patient. The supervisor/supervisee relationship is not unlike the resident/patient relationship in that it focuses on the interactions and the personal antecedents which influence those interactions. Such a statement might suggest that supervision constitutes treatment of the resident. Perhaps. But only if therapy is understood as enhancement of the individual and not simply as eradication of psychopathology. On the other hand, residents in psychiatry are liable to mental and emotional disorders as are others. Supervision should be sensitive to the manifestation of psychiatric disorder in trainees since its principal functions are the implementation of psychological well-being and the development of psychological fulfillment of the trainee. The acquisition of knowledge is not dependent upon supervision but is facilitated therein nonetheless. Supervision binds together acquired knowledge, psychological health, and fulfillment in a well integrated mental health professional. Such a state is not attained without anguish.

TRAINING ISSUES FOR THE PSYCHIATRY RESIDENT

The development of the psychiatrist is a complex endeavor. Throughout the residency the trainee comes to know discouragement, depression, and anxiety. Behind these experiences lie a wide variety of events and circumstances that put the training process in jeopardy. Personal problems bring individualistic challenges peculiar to each resident. Although these challenges might be problematic at one level they are events that offer opportunity for development. Some residents manage their training experiences better than others but most come to know some degree of anxiety during their development. Three areas appear to be especially troublesome for most residents at one time or another during their training: identity, issues, psychological thinking, and legitimacy of purpose.

IDENTITY ISSUES

During the course of medical school education, students begin to evolve a sense of professional identity and begin to think of themselves as physicians. Many of the significant people in their lives begin to respond to them with respect, admiration and even awe. The medical student's family begins to cast him or her in heroic proportions. Even the faculty begin to express themselves with a growing sense of comradeship as the student moves into the clinical years. For the medical student, the acquisition of the doctorate degree represents a supreme accomplishment. Not only is there a sense of fullfillment but also a spirit of promise of things yet to be. The new physician entering a residency in medicine, surgery, or obstetrics must evolve a professional identity as must the resident in psychiatry. For the latter, the lines of authority are less clear and the resident frequently sees his or her role as ambiguous and poorly defined. Most psychiatric training programs are built around team treatment models, wherein the resident sees a number of other mental health professionals participating in the determination of clinical goals and objectives. Since the nurse, psychologist, and social worker have treatment skills, the resident in psychiatry sees considerable threat to his or her role as the decision maker in determining treatment goals. Moreover, the resident in psychiatry is frequently reminded by others that psychiatry is not a science and that psychiatrists therefore are not legitimate physicians. Other members of the psychiatric treatment team are not able to prescribe medications and their treatment interests are more inclined toward psychotherapy rather than toward medical treatment that might include the use of drugs. Furthermore, even some psychiatrists disdain the use of psychopharmacologic treatment, thereby causing the resident to either undervalue his medical skills or to become defensive about his role in the treatment of the patient. It is not unusual for the resident in psychiatry to experience difficulty with other members of the treatment team regarding this role and to feel disparaged by others.

In addition to the struggle for self-esteem, the resident in psychiatry must also evolve that sense of being a psychiatrist in the best meaning of the title. With the evolving of his professional identity, the resident is exposed to a welter of theoretical concepts that initially tend to be overwhelming. Native skills and assets ordinarily available to him or her become sorely tested by feelings of inadequacy as the resident struggles to evolve a philosophical approach to this new and emerging profession. Being a psychiatrist has little meaning for the trainee in his or her early development. Indeed, there might yet remain some negative connotations about psychiatry extant from medical school experience. It is particularly difficult to pursue eagerly a professional identity which appears obscure and ill-defined. It is difficult to be what one does not yet comprehend. Around this issue of professional identity clusters considerable anxiety. Other training issues conspire with the search for professional identity to compound the anxiety.

PSYCHOLOGICAL THINKING

All professions and specialties develop idiosyncratic communications understood by disciples but poorly comprehended by the nondevout. Surgery and medicine utilize myriad abbreviations, surnamed syndromes, and procedures fully understood and usefully employed by the practitioners. Psychiatry and psychology speak a special language and use words unknown to the uninitiated. Thus, trainees experience a language gap at the beginning of their training. The resident in psychiatry faces the same barrier but is doubly disadvantaged as he or she begins to struggle for mastery of the process of psychological thinking. The resident is bewildered by the observations of teachers as they delineate subleties and nuances found in the scrutiny of patient interactions and communications. While observing the content of patient communication, the trainee feels confused as others discuss the process of communication. As others glean the hidden meanings and meta-communications of his or her patients, the resident in psychiatry begins to feel lost and confused. Dynamic formulations that postulate sets of psychological possibilities or the genesis of present neurotic manifestation lead the trainee into a state of confusion and anxiety. The trainee who possesses a facile capacity for psychological thinking finds the training process less confusing and less anxiety-laden. One must be able to avoid the allure of detail at the expense of global impressions while understanding the implication of seemingly innocuous happenings. The trainee must evolve special thinking processes which free one from the tyrannies of sequential logic. The trainee must be able to tolerate ambiguity and to endure a dysfunction of cause and effect. The understanding of human behavior requires well-disciplined observation of not only the spoken word but also the subtle shifts in tonal quality as well as shifts in body position. The trainee must seek and understand the contradictions that can exist between stated motivation and manifest behavior. Paradox, contradiction, and ambiguity seem constant companions to the resident as he or she attempts to develop a sense of psychological thinking. This is one of the major sources of anxiety for the developing mental health professional and represents a major obstacle in that development.

Coupled with the struggle for competence in psychologic thinking is the flooding of the trainee with a welter of theoretical concepts designed to explain human thinking and behavior. Psychiatry still lacks the conceptual silver bullet for the understanding and treatment of mental illness. Indeed the trainee is often overcome with diverse theoretical concepts, some of which are entirely antithetical to others. Compounding the pain associated with the development of psychological thinking is the loss of once reliable and cherished concepts of simple cause and effect. No longer does the resident find himself or herself surrounded by familiar landmarks. This new endeavor lacks the clarity of categoric description. Human behavior is not predictable and emotion is not quantifiable. The resident in psychiatry recalls the certainty of measurable physical illness and wonders if he or she has made the right decision.

LEGITIMACY OF PURPOSE

The third area of anxiety for the resident in psychiatry tends to develop later in the training period rather than early because it requires disillusionment. The haunting question for the resident is the legitimacy of his profession. It would be wrong to suggest that other branches of medicine never know doubt and uncertainty. Discouragement becomes a frequent companion to the physician who struggles to preserve life. Other branches of medicine have reason to question the value of what they do for their patients, but the resident in psychiatry comes to know a special kind of disillusionment and questioning of purpose. After some of the other issues of training are beginning to resolve, the resident in psychiatry begins to wonder if what he does makes any real difference. Although psychiatry has made great strides in understanding and treating mental illness, we still lack a real understanding of the cause or the cure. Great numbers of people have been sent from the institutions of asylum although their mental illness shows no sign of diminution. New drugs have helped reduce the disability, but specifics defy us. Psychoanalysis has contributed more to the understanding of human psychic life than any other endeavor. Yet a sure way of bringing brotherhood and understanding to the human race eludes us. Behaviorism has made great contributions to the understanding of human actions but has yet to stem the effects of severe mental illness. Moreover, the inability of psychiatry to devise reliable and predictable treatment for schizophrenia, alcohol and drug addictions, severe character disorders, and Alzheimer's Disease, as well as the debilitation of senility compels one to question the effectiveness of what we do. The resident in psychiatry comes to know the discouragement of long and difficult treatment that ends in suicide, or the autistic child who never comes to share a feeling of life with another human being. When a patient willfully takes his life, there comes to the physician a unique pain that is particularly difficult to contemplate, fear, or experience. Perhaps the most destructive anxiety is the one which clusters about the legitimacy of our work. Most of all, the role of the supervisory process finds itself well-tested in this crucial area of the development of the psychiatrist.

Professional and life experience of the supervisor is the guiding force throughout the training experience of the resident and provides opportunities to work through the anxieties of professional growth. The supervisory process leads to professional growth for the supervisor as well as the supervisee. The process will be greatly influenced by the theoretical orientation of the supervisor as will be his or her life, for it is within the structure of that orientation that the supervisor evolves his/her own personal and professional development. The supervisory process comes under the influence of the supervisor's life and in consequence the professional and personal development of the supervisee is similarly influenced. Most psychiatric residents have been in continuous education since entering school. Early in the life of the candidate for medical school there is a sense of mission even though the goal of that mission is not yet known. Qualifications for graduate/professional schools are stringent and although the future successful candidates do not yet see their destiny clearly, they nonetheless begin to understand early in life that they have special talents and skills, and that these qualities impel them toward special goals. Certainly as early as adolescence, and perhaps sooner, the ultimately successful candidate begins to discern the direction of this personal mission. If one is to be a successful candidate for medical school the student must conduct life in a specific manner and the accomplishments of adolescence must conform to the fulfillment of that destiny. Most successful candidates to medical school had an adolescence different from the average adolescent. Many of the conflicts of adolescence are addressed by the candidate in a fashion most conducive to the fulfillment of that destiny with the result being an incomplete resolution of those conflicts. Moreover, these adolescents will tend to deal with their conflicts in ways characteristic of the more conscientious and somewhat obsessive/compulsive personality. There is a subverting of these conflicts in pursuit of higher goals. Preparation for and the completion of medical school offers little opportunity for major psychic-energy investment in the resolution of adolescent conflicts; nor does the process of separation permit much in the way of personal life problems. Even where the process permits, the individual does not allow. The young physician begins post-graduate training in a context of unresolved issues surrounding emancipation and identity. They have endured a special brand of dependency that, on the one hand, requires a sense of great responsibility in the management of life and death events in the lives of their patients, while on the other hand, they may be unable to assume complete responsibility for their own lives.

The supervisor brings to the process of supervision a broader data base of human experience than does the supervisee but has shared many of the same constraints in his or her own development. It is in the recognition and understanding of these constraints where the supervisor is able to help the supervisee move not only toward an understanding of human development but also toward his or her own growth. Only to the extent that the supervisor has effected his own emancipation and has moved toward a firming of his own identity as parts of a well-integrated ego can he or she fulfill the role of supervisor. Only to the extent that the supervisee is able to acquire knowledge of normal and abnormal behavior and to discover and begin to resolve those constraints on his or her own development can the supervisee fully benefit from the supervisory process. Once initiated, this growth must continue to the full integration of the ego for the supervisor and the supervisee.

Learning and Teaching Psychotherapy: Signposts and Growth Stages

Robert P. Archer
Tom H. Peake

> There are two kinds of patients; those we help and those we learn from.
>
> —F. Fromm-Reichman

This chapter proposes that there are meaningful passages through which a student of psychotherapy may become a competent and knowledgeable psychotherapist. Before describing a series of developmental stages, however, it is useful to acknowledge the shortcomings of any developmental model of the learning and teaching of psychotherapy. First, the division of any developmental process into discrete or semi-discrete stages is ultimately arbitrary in operation and based upon value-laden assumptions. Stated differently, the creation of stages is always arbitrary in terms of what the writer chooses as the end of one stage and the beginning of another, and the creation is value-laden in terms of what concepts, behaviors, and expectancies the writer underscores in the selection of salient stages. Further, developmental stages or a developmental view may be taken in relation to almost any learning process. One might create stages of development for an experience as comprehensive as that of adult life (Sheehy, 1976) or for an experience as specific and time-restricted as the internship for clinical psychologists (Lamb, Baker, Jennings, & Yarris, 1982). In providing a description of the internship "passages" for example, Lamb et al. (1982) included the following developmental stages: (1) preentry, which includes application acceptance and attendant apprehension, (2) early intern syndrome, including information gathering and finding a place in the agency, (3) intern identity, which focuses on the realization of strengths, limitations, self-doubt, and greater role differentiation,

(4) the emerging professional with an increased sense of competence, and (5) resolution, which includes separation from the agency. The utility or viability of creation of any developmental model for a particular task must ultimately rest upon the degree to which such concepts aid the teaching and learning process.

Given the complexity and confusion surrounding the role of the psychotherapist, it is not surprising that there have been very few attempts to delineate the developmental processes involved in reaching competence in the psychotherapy area. Strupp (1974) noted that while much has been written concerning the structure and curriculum of professional training in the mental health disciplines, we have tended to ignore the specifics of the learning process including issues related to the personal development of the psychotherapy student. Recently, Ralph (1980) offered a developmental perspective on the process of learning psychotherapy which shall be used as an anchoring point for this chapter. While Ralph's concepts may be more applicable to insight-oriented psychotherapies than to the behavioral orientations, his article nevertheless serves as an innovative and stimulating view valuable to students and teachers across the spectrum of schools of psychotherapies. Ralph defines developmental milestones in the learning process of psychotherapy as "radical changes in perspective" of what defines and characterizes the therapy process for the clinician in training. Further, Ralph presents a developmental continuum from "concrete and common sense conceptions of psychotherapy" to increasingly more abstract and introspective notions of what constitutes therapy and treatment. Thus, as the psychotherapist gains maturity and experience, what are viewed as relevant tasks for both the therapist and the patient tend to change in nature and perspective.

While it is widely recognized that psychotherapy is an extremely demanding and complex activity, little has been written about the specific stresses experienced by the psychotherapist in his or her development. Frieda Fromm-Reichmann (1950) has written, "Patients tend towards health, and they are lonely. Their wish for help, their tendency towards health, and their loneliness are much more important to them than the chronological or professional age of the person to whom they turn for aid," (p. 13). While this statement may offer solace and comfort to the beginning psychotherapist in terms of the nature of the demands placed upon them by their patients, it does not address the self-demands frequently generated by psychotherapists. One of the major stress points for the beginning psychotherapist relates to the scientific challenge of the field of psychotherapy.

Perry London (1964) has suggested that psychotherapists are members of the "secular priesthood" who draw upon scientific methodology and knowledge to offer treatment to distressed individuals in the same manner that religious functionaries draw upon biblical and divine powers to offer counsel and guidance to distressed believers. Specifically, London has stated "psychotherapists must finally appeal to science to justify their activity, just as ministers must appeal to Revelation," (p. 163). This concept may be seen as compatible with the Scientist-Practitioner model for training of clinical psychologists, which views the psychologist as a generator and consumer of scientifically derived knowledge about people upon which treatment interventions are based and modified. Clearly then, this model views the psychologist as first and foremost a generator and consumer of science. It would appear clear that the appeal to scientific knowledge also serves as the basis for the practices of the psychiatrist and social worker as noted in the previous chapters by Orvin and Triezenberg. This is not to imply that the scientific model is a particularly comfortable one for practitioners of psychotherapy. Within all mental health fields there are individuals who articulately argue that psychotherapy is not a science but an "art." Meltzoff and Kornreich (1970) have noted, however, "To come full circle, to maintain that psychotherapy is not a science but an art neither explains, justifies, nor excuses anything," (p. 8). The position that psychotherapy is an "art," taken to imply that neither the skills nor the effects of psychotherapy are predictable, reproducible, or objective, is clearly a minority position among clinical practitioners, theorists, and consumers of psychotherapy. Given the perspective that the psychotherapist is grounded in and evaluated by scientific methodology, there are numerous stress points inherent in this approach which create anxiety and insecurity for the therapist in training.

ART AND SCIENCE: THE LIMITS OF KNOWLEDGE

Within the field of psychology, graduate students in clinical psychology frequently find themselves under attack by their colleagues in the experimental psychologies who may claim that the practice of psychotherapy is "irresponsible" until such time as scientifically validated treatment methodologies may be demonstrated. The division within the field of scientific psychology was noted by Cronbach in 1957 in his presidential address to the American Psychological Association. Cronbach argued that there are two historical streams of method and thought within the field of psychology, one discipline consisting of experimental psychology in which the scientist manipulates or modifies conditions in order to observe their consequences, and the other field of correlational psychology in which the investigator takes advantage of existing variations between individuals and groups to examine associations with dependent variables of interest. Cronbach noted that the experimental method allows for rigorous tests of hypotheses and confident statements about causation, whereas the correlational method serves to study what "man has not learned to control or can never hope to control," (1957, p. 672). Cronbach strongly argued that these two disciplines of scientific psychology must be combined into one common approach utilizing one common methodology to achieve a more comprehensive understanding of human behavior. Despite the nearly 30 years that have transpired since Cronbach's address, this task is as necessary today as it was in 1957.

In addition to those individuals who challenge the scientific status of psychotherapy, the developing clinician is also subject to challenges concerning the utility of a scientific approach to understanding human behavior and treating human problems. Yalom (1980) has noted, "again and again one encounters a basic fact of life in psychotherapy research: the precision of the result is directly proportional to the triviality of the variables studied. A strange type of science!" (p. 24). Yalom futher suggests that psychotherapy research has had very minimal impact on the actual practice of clinicians, and he quotes Carl Rogers' observation that not even psychotherapy researchers alter their own psychotherapy based on empirical findings. While the Scientist-Practitioner model would imply that psychotherapists' select their psychotherapy techniques based upon thoughtful reviews of the scientific literature, Cummings and Lucchese (1978) have noted that the adoption of a psychological orientation typically is a function of accidental factors and unconscious influences rather than rational and scientific processes. Added to this dilemma is a recent article by Watts (1980) who postulates that clinical judgment may sometimes be adversely affected by the products of clinical training. Specifically Watts notes that clinical training may lead to relatively high risk strategies of judgment which tend to divert attention away from more objective "low risk judgments and interventions within the clinical situation." Quite recently, Koch (1981) has taken direct aim at the concept of psychology as an "independent, experimental science." Koch concludes that psychology's claim to an independent and scientific status has been, at best, misguided and, "in consequence, much of psychological history may be seen as a form of scientific role playing which, however sophisticated, entails the trivialization, and even evasion, of significant problems" (p. 257).

In summarizing these articles, it is apparent that students of psychotherapy may well be left feeling insecure, pessimistic, and uncertain regarding the scientific underpinnings of this discipline, both from the viewpoint of the legitimacy as well as the utility of their claims of a scientific understanding of human behavior. If the students attempt to circumvent this dilemma by seeking refuge in the view that psychotherapy is an art, they are scarcely on more stable grounds given their novice status in attempting to practice this "art form." They may well be left with a deep-seated conviction of their inadequacy as both scientists and practitioners. They must struggle with issues concerning what they are ultimately attempting to do, the choosing of the way in which they are attempting to do it, and evaluating the effectiveness of their efforts. Ultimately, these questions may boil down to the issue: Is what I'm trying to do effective and, if so, am I an individual who can do it effectively? Having reviewed the stress points in the development of the psychotherapist, we may now use this as a backdrop from which to explore Ralph's (1980) four stages of the developmental process.

Growing With the Limits of Knowledge

Ralph (1980) describes the first stage or milestone in the developmental process of the novice clinician as, "learning the role of psychotherapist as a non-directive expert." Ralph defines this stage by the therapist's perception of his role as that of providing authoritative and definitive solutions and advice to the patient. Thus, psychotherapy during this stage is viewed as the provision of concrete and tangible wisdom to the patient. Ralph draws an analogy between this view and the traditional perspective of the role of the physician who collects specific facts from the patients (i.e., signs and symptoms of disease) and prescribes a tangible intervention (e.g., a medication to be taken on a particular schedule for a particular problem). This perspective is also congruent with a literal and concrete interpretation of the Scientist-Practitioner model. Here the beginning therapist may assume that after listening to the patient's presenting complaints, the primary task is to return to the scientific journals, examine statistical tests of significance for particular psychotherapy outcomes, and select the most recent, relevant and appropriate intervention for the treatment of the disorder. At this stage of practice, the clinician is largely atheoretical beyond the conviction that his or her role is that of an expert prepared to "fix" human dilemmas.

In the second developmental milestone for the aspiring clinician, Ralph suggests that the student adopts a theoretical approach in an undifferentiated and concrete fashion. Therapy at this stage is viewed as a content-centered and patient-centered activity in which the goal of therapy is to "figure out" the patient within the context of a theoretical model and, based upon this detective work, to lead the patient back to health through the administration of "pearls of wisdom" sprinkled generously by the therapist during the therapeutic hour. Ralph notes that at this stage of development psychotherapists frequently take refuge in a Rogerian and nondirective stance. It can be noted, however, that the dogmatic adherence to some form of psychotherapy (e.g., Skinnerian, Analytic, Gestalt) is a hallmark at this stage of development. As a defense against the therapists' own anxieties, rigid adherence to a particular psychotherapeutic model may provide a temporary sense of relief. Meltzoff and Kornreich (1970) have noted "new therapeutic approaches generate tremendous initial enthusiasm and attract loyal cohorts. Ardor, fervor, and conviction are mighty lieutenants in the missionary cause. Clinicians who are short on tools and long on difficult cases make good converts," (p. 64). For psychologists, this rigidity may be seen not only in the use of psychotherapeutic techniques but even in the assessment tools selected for evaluating the patient. Thus, the graduate student may exclusively and consistently select the MMPI for personality evaluation rather than the Rorschach (or vice versa), without fully understanding the relative benefits and utilities of either instrument. Others may disdain traditional assessment entirely based on strictly held behavioral beliefs. Similar to the prior stage of development, the inclusion of the therapists' feelings and responses are not viewed as relevant material for consideration in the therapeutic process. Indeed, the process of psychotherapy is largely ignored with the therapists' attention being focused upon the content of the patients' statements without attention to nonverbal communications or shifts in feeling states manifested by the patient.

The third stage of the development of the psychotherapist is viewed by Ralph as a "relationship-centered" approach that involves the discovery of psychotherapy as an interpersonal process. The therapist gradually moves from the content of the patient's verbalizations to the interpersonal process as the main focus of his or her attention during the therapy hour, that is, to the feelings and emotions that are occurring between the patient and the therapist. Thus, attention is given to the issues of transference and countertransference as conceptualized within dynamically-oriented psychotherapies. At this stage, value may be placed on such concepts as Sullivan's "participant-observer" notion in which the therapist is simultaneously an intimate part of the relationship process as well as a critical observer of events within the psychotherapeutic hour. Perhaps most importantly, it is at this stage of development that the therapist begins to view his or her mastery and competence as a process of continual personal growth that extends beyond technical skill acquisition and may continue over the lifetime of the practice of the psychotherapist.

Provocatively, Ralph postulates the final stage of development of the psychotherapist as a "therapist-centered" approach in which there is increasing awareness of both the utility and the limitations of the therapist's feelings. As the therapist develops an increased sense of confidence and self-esteem, his or her own reactions become more than a source of anxiety and are viewed as an important fund of information about the therapeutic process. Thus, the therapist at this stage begins to focus upon learning to use the self as a primary psychotherapeutic tool. This viewpoint might be expressed by Carl Whitaker's comments that his primary goal within family therapy sessions is to reach a point in the therapeutic process where he feels safe, comfortable, and productive. By this comment, Whitaker is suggesting that if the therapist is able to merge with the family system successfully, then his or her experience of the therapeutic hour should be reflective of the family system's experience in general. Therefore, if the therapist within the family context is feeling comfortable, relaxed, and productive then this serves as the most vital piece of information indicating the outcome of the family therapy process. Ralph is also careful to note that at this stage of development the therapist begins to wrestle with issues regarding the limitations that his or her feelings impose on their practice of psychotherapy. Thus, entailed in the knowledge of the therapist's own countertransference responses is the understanding that unresolved issues pertaining to the therapist's own development may serve to prevent that therapist from rendering effective treatment to particular patients. At the very least, a therapist at this stage of development should be carefully monitoring issues of contertransference. The therapist may frequently seek out personal psychotherapy to aid in clarifying salient issues in his or her own development or begin to draw heavily upon prior therapy experiences in terms of his or her own current treatment efforts with patients.

Doehrman (1976) describes the concept of *parallel process* in supervision. The student therapists' difficulties in learning involve their own character attitudes and ego-defenses. As long as the trainees' difficulties in learning therapy parallel the patients' conflictual issues in therapy, these problems are not narrowly defined as impediments to learning that should be eliminated. Rather they are the very vehicle through which therapeutic progress may be effected. This subtle technique of supervision seems to be more fully appreciated in Ralph's later stage of learning psychotherapy. As one might imagine, the technique comes as quite a shock if imposed on a student too early in their training.

We began the discussion of developmental stages in learning psychotherapy by suggesting that a developmental perspective has utility to the degree that it aids in the process of acquiring and teaching a particular set of skills. Ralph notes that beyond a warm and supportive environment necessary for the acquisition of therapy skills, an awareness of the student's level of development allows for the matching of supervision approach to the student's needs. Thus, Ralph implies that psychotherapy supervision with a central focus on process issues and parallel process may be overwhelming for the novice psychotherapy student who views psychotherapy as providing "expert" advice to the client. This point may be exemplified in a recent study by Worthington and Roehlke (1979) who surveyed 31 beginning practicum counselors and 42 supervisors in terms of their perception in psychotherapy supervision. Whereas supervisors perceived supervision as primarily a process of providing feedback to the supervisees concerning their counseling approach and ability, beginning counselors found that supervision was most beneficial when supervisors directly taught skills used in counseling and when supervision sessions were highly structured. The differences in these perceptions of psychotherapy supervision might be a reflection of the differences in maturation and development present between beginning counseling students and experienced practicum supervisors.

IMPLICATIONS OF A DEVELOPMENTAL CONCEPT

How does a supervisor attempt to match his or her supervision style to the needs and abilities of the novice clinician? The complexity of this topic is intimidating to even the most brave or foolhardy writers. Putting aside the issues of the focus of supervision, there are obviously numerous formats through which psychotherapy supervision may be offered. Vandermay and Peake (1980) have noted that the formats of supervision may include: (a) process reports or recalls by the trainee, (b) audiotape, (c) videotape, (d) one-way mirror viewing, (e) co-therapy with the supervisor, (f) group or seminar supervision of several trainees with the supervisor, or (g) various combinations of the above. Moving to the issues of styles or focus of the supervision process, Wagner (1957) divides methods of supervision into three types: (a) *patient-centered,* in which the focus of supervision is on technical problems experienced by the therapist with the patient and about which the supervisor offers advice to the therapist; (b) *therapist-centered,* in which the supervision focus rests upon the therapist's countertransference reactions and the degree to which the therapist's responses tend to influence the therapeutic process; and (c) *process-centered,* in which the emphasis is on the interaction between the therapist and the patient but also may include the process that is occurring between the therapist and his or her supervisor. Doehrman (1976) has termed this latter style of supervision *parallel process* in supervision, in which dynamics experienced in one relationship affect and are reflected in the other relationship. In this approach to supervision, the therapist's problems in supervision are related to the patient's problems in psychotherapy and vice versa.

Having thus conceptualized a small number of the ways in which the focus and formats of psychotherapy may be viewed, the question remains in what way this process may be maximized, based upon a developmental perspective. The authors humbly suggest two considerations that may aid in this task: (a) the value of an explicit understanding between the supervisor and supervisee concerning the focus of psychotherapy, and (b) the utility of multidimensional supervision.

SUPERVISION CONTRACTS

When seasoned psychotherapists exchange stories of their most disastrous treatment cases, a central issue frequently underlying these experiences is a therapist-patient misunderstanding concerning the nature of the therapeutic contract. It might also be suggested that a frequent cause of nonproductivity and adversive reactions in psychotherapy supervision is the lack of an explicit understanding or contract between the supervisor and supervisee concerning the format and style of supervision. The lack of this explicit contract may often reflect a poor recognition or awareness of the state of the student's development. A beginning clinician who expects to receive concrete advice and direction concerning psychotherapy may feel threatened and confused, and thus act defensively, when unexpectedly confronted with a supervisor who wishes to discuss countertransference issues. Similarly, a supervisee who has begun to deal with issues concerning his or her own feelings and responses in the therapy process may be bored and respond with disinterest to supervision concentrating on the patient-centered case material. The view that both the supervisor and supervisee should explicitly negotiate the basis of their supervision entails more than just a recommendation for clarification during the first session of supervision. Rather, as is frequently of great utility in psychotherapy (Goldstein, 1962), the psychotherapy supervision process should also include periodic reviews of the supervisor's and supervisee's expectations about evaluation, scope of focus, and level of integration. The supervision should be subject to modification based upon the changing needs involved in this complex process. While the development of an explicit contract between supervisor and supervisee concerning the format and content of supervision may not ensure productive work, it does tend to minimize the potential for disastrous experiences marked by frustration, anger, anxiety and disinterest. The contract also allows evaluation to be based upon dimensions agreed upon in advance rather than dimensions discovered after the fact.

Multi-level Supervision

The second recommendation for enhancing the process of psychotherapy supervision concerns the use of multidimensional or multi-level supervision. This concept rests upon the belief that optimal supervision may entail the use of a supervisory style which involves comments from the supervisor that may be utilized by the supervisee at a number of levels. Related to this notion, Bruno Bettelheim (1976) has discussed the intense interest in fairy tales displayed by children across generations, based on the tales' ability to serve as metaphors for human experience useful to the child across a variety of levels, from the concrete to the abstract. Similarly, Eric Berne (1972) examined the utility of common fairy tales such as Little Red Riding Hood and the Story of Sleeping Beauty in terms of their metaphoric value for common human experiences and dilemmas. Thus, fairy tales and folklore myths may be taken at any level—from the concrete level of an entertaining story that holds the attention of a young child to the level of an analogy or metaphor of human experience. These metaphors can be understood in a manner that illuminates complex human dilemmas including the psychotherapeutic process itself.

As an extension of this concept of symbols useful at multiple levels of awareness, Michael Barnat (1977) has written of the use of spontaneous supervisory metaphors as a way of communicating important material to supervisees in a manner that tends to minimize trainee anxiety. The author provides multiple examples of the use of spontaneous metaphor in clinical supervision. Among these examples, Barnat illustrates his point by relating an experience he had early in training in which he performed a psychiatric intake on a female client. Barnat (1977) noted,

> Both of us were anxious and self-conscious, though the intake involved the appropriate history taking. The sexual nature of our anxiety was clear at the end of the tense hour when she asked me for my phone number. Having no presence of mind at the moment I gave it to her. The session left me feeling exploited, excited, and angry with my own vulnerability. After an embarrassing group supervision session during which this issue was explored, the supervisor underscored the meaning of the moment by asking, "do you think you can get your number back?" (p. 312)

As eloquently noted by Barnat, this metaphorical instruction could be utilized by him at several levels. At the most concrete level, it was an instruction to the therapist for specific action to physically take back possession of his telephone number. At a more complex and abstract level, it was a suggestion to the therapist that he could recover his adequacy and mastery within the psychotherapy supervision by paying attention to his areas of vulnerabilities, i.e., that it was possible to recover one's sense of competence and purpose. For the beginning therapist at a relatively concrete stage, the metaphoric directive would have tended to reduce anxiety and provide for immediate action, while for the more advanced student it would have focused upon issues of therapy process and countertransference forces.

In summary, the concept of multi-level supervision is an extension of the concept of matching the supervision format and style to the supervisee's needs and level of conceptualizations. Its intriguing implication is that while good supervision may consist of specifically matching the level of supervision to the student's needs, perhaps the most illuminating moments in psychotherapy supervision come from supervisors who are skilled enough (and perhaps intuitive enough) to offer supervisory comments which may work on a number of levels to aid the therapist in his or her personal development and growth.

CONCLUSIONS

It is hoped that this discussion will facilitate the supervisor and supervisee in tailoring and structuring the parameters of therapy supervision. It is suggested that this structuring entail a dialogue to encompass: (1) an assessment of the student's level of professional development to include both technical skill level and conceptual and personal development; (2) a clarification of the scope of topic areas to be covered in and excluded from supervision (e.g., Where does countertransference consideration end and therapy with the student begin?); (3) a consideration of ways in which a wide variance in theoretical orientations may hinder or help the process; (4) a discussion of the ways that personality styles of the participants may influence the process; and (5) a clarification of how and when evaluation will be accomplished or feedback will be provided.

While psychotherapy supervision is a crucial process both to the education of mental health professionals and to the care of their patients or clients, it has suffered from a lack of theoretical and research attention. In the absence of explicit attention, choices of supervision style and approach have been largely a product of tradition. In other words, we are most likely to "do it as it was done to us." For those supervisors who were blessed by creative supervision as trainees, this implicit system may hold advantages, but for those less fortunate it leads to a repetition of errors. It is hoped that by focusing explicit attention on the complexities of supervision, the process will be improved. The model provided by Ralph (1980) is only one of many useful views that could be generated to better understand the psychotherapy supervision experience. Such theoretical model development is a crucial task at this point in our understanding of the clinical supervisory process. Developmental conceptualizations clarify the growth process in learning the scientific craft of psychotherapy. If a supervisor is aware of such models and applies them judiciously, the teaching and learning of psychotherapy benefits.

REFERENCES

Barnat, M. R. Spontaneous supervisory metaphor in the resolution of trainee anxiety. *Professional Psychology,* 1977, *8,* 307-315.

Berne, E. *What do you say after you say hello?* New York: Bantam Books, 1973.

Bettelheim, B. *The uses of enchantment: The meaning and importance of fairy tales.* New York: Vintage Books, 1976.

Cronbach, L. J. The two disciplines of scientific psychology. *American Psychologist,* 1957, *12,* 671-684.

Cummings, N., & Lucchese, G. Adoption of a psychological orientation: The role of the inadvertent. *Psychotherapy: Theory, Research and Practice,* 1978, *15,* 323-328.

Doehrman, M. J. G. Parallel processes in supervision of psychotherapy. *Bulletin of Menninger Clinic,* 1976, *40,* 71-84.

Fromm-Reichmann, F. *Principals of intensive psychotherapy.* Chicago: University of Chicago Press, 1950.

Goldstein, A. P., *Therapist-patient expectancies in psychotherapy.* New York: Pergamon Press, 1962.

Koch, S. The nature and limits of psychological knowledge: Lessons of a century qua "science." *American Psychologist,* 1957, *12,* 671-684.

Lamb, D.H., Baker, J.M., Jennings, M.I., & Yarris, E. Passages of an internship. *Professional Psychology,* 1982, *13,* 661-669.

London, P. *The modes and morals of psychotherapy.* New York: Holt, Rinehart and Winston, 1964.

Meltzoff, J., & Kornreich, M. *Research in psychotherapy.* New York: Atherton Press, 1970.

Ralph, N.B. Learning Psychotherapy: A developmental perspective. *Psychiatry,* 1980, *43,* 243-250.

Sheehy, G. *Passages: Predictable crises of adult life.* New York: Dutton, 1976.

Strupp, H. Graduate training in clinical psychology: A very personal endeavor. *Journal of Clinical Psychology,* 1974, *28,* 1-2.

Vandermay, J., & Peake, T. Psychodrama as a psychotherapy supervision technique. *Group Psychotherapy, Psychodrama, and Sociometry,* 1980, *33,* 25-32.

Wagner, F. F. Supervision of psychotherapy. *American Journal of Psychotherapy,* 1957, *11,* 759-768.

Watts, F. N. Clinical judgment and clinical training. *British Journal of Medical Psychology,* 1980, *53,* 95-108.

Worthington, E. L., & Roehlke, H. J. Effective supervision as perceived by beginning counselors in training. *Journal of Counseling Psychology,* 1979, *26,* 64-73.

PROBLEMS AND OPPORTUNITIES OF PROFESSIONAL GROWTH

Hazardous Assumptions

Merville O. Vincent

This edition is written primarily with the psychotherapist in mind. Thus, the context is based on experience and research with psychiatrists, social workers, and psychologists. This writer's background involves dealing primarily with physicians; physicians who have developed psychiatric difficulties.

Many of the problems faced by the medical clinician are faced with minor variations by the social worker and the psychologist in clinical practice. Because I believe it is wiser to write from one's own experience than to write beyond one's experience, I will direct my thoughts primarily to physicians. I will request social workers, psychologists and other counselors to heed those principles that seem applicable to their own lives and practices.

A pattern of morbidity has become apparent among physicians who are not handling stress well (A'Brook, Hailstone, & McLauchlan, 1967; Murray, 1974; Sakinofsky, 1980; Vailant, Brighton, & McArthur, 1970). Some of the consequences of maladaptation are overwork, fatigue, depression, burnout, a high incidence of alcohol and drug-abuse, marital breakdown, and unnecessarily high rates of suicide.

Why is this so? Perhaps one aspect of the problem is that in the training and life of clinicians the focus is on others, the needs of patients or clients. Physicians who develop problems have often lived as if they did not have ordinary human needs and conflicts—needs such as security, self-esteem, to be liked, intimacy, rest, and recreation. Graduate school puts similar pressures on nonphysician therapists. Being in a helping role with people at times of crisis involves stresses not experienced in many occupations. While most physicians appear to handle the many stresses well, a significant number do not. Journal articles in recent years have shown a great preoccupation by the caring professions with the topic of burnout in their own ranks. In exploring the causes of failure to adapt to the stresses of clinical practice, the focus is usually on the two areas of personal vulnerability and the stresses that are inevitable in the practice of medicine.

I propose to focus primarily on a third area, the stresses that we impose on ourselves unnecessarily by certain "hazardous assumptions." These are underlying assumptions or personal constructs that influence our decisions, actions, and feelings. These assumptions often convert the inevitable hazards of being a physician into the *preventable disasters* that some physicians experience. Some of these assumptions are conscious thoughts that guide the physician; others are assumptions at an unconscious or pre-conscious level that direct his or her actions. These assumptions are critical, not only in how they influence decisions, actions, and feelings, but also in how they influence information-processing of reality. Many psychotherapeutic efforts center around the correction of misconceptions. In fact, cognitive therapy is based on the theory that an individual's feelings and behavior are largely determined by the way in which one structures the world. Therefore, it is important for the clinician to be aware of how he or she structures his or her own world. In this context, I would like to look at a number of hazardous assumptions that I believe lead to maladaptation.

HAZARDOUS ASSUMPTIONS LEADING TO MALADAPTATION

1. Assume That Your Role is to Stamp Out Disease, Suffering, and Death

This guarantees constant defeat and therefore role strain. In an effort to win in this battle, some doctors run faster than other doctors, work harder, get more fatigued, and develop more despair and guilt.

The concept of the role of the physician often has been discussed and clarified in medical school. Largely by the process of osmosis from the faculty, the developing doctor begins to conceive his or her role as one to stamp out disease, suffering, and death. Later in practice, when surrounded by these, the physician feels like a failure. This feeling can contribute to patterns of overwork (to prove one's self) fatigue, and despair, which all too readily may be alleviated by alcohol or drugs. The clinician needs a reasonable understanding both of his or her own role and of the limits of medicine. The profession's inability to stamp out either cancer or schizophrenia should not be perceived as a personal failure by the practicing physician.

Healthy adaptation is more likely where one's role is defined as "to cure sometimes, to relieve often, and to comfort always." This role is broader than stamping out disease, suffering, and death. It is also to help bear disease, suffering, and death.

2. Assume Your Goal and the Patient's Expectations Are the Same

Patients hope for ease when the reality is disease. Patients hope for health when the reality is sickness. Patients hope for life when the reality is death. Do not be surprised and hurt when, after your best efforts, patients are angry because their expectations have not been met. Depending on how your anger is handled, you may begin to feel inadequate, guilty, and depressed, or alternatively, get very angry at the "ungrateful wretches" you have as patients.

To prevent problems in the doctor-patient relationship, it is important to be clear about your role with this particular patient, with this particular disease and unique problems. Patients with terminal illness and chronic debilitating illness hope for life and ease. They often become angry at God, fate, doctors, and nurses. The anger of the patient directed to the doctor may cause the doctor to feel guilty and inadequate, which may result in excessive tests or excessive treatments. Thus both the physician and the patient suffer. Alternatively, the patient's misplaced and displaced anger may cause the physician to feel angry and become rejecting in his behavior toward the patient. Again, both the physician and patient suffer. Appropriate handling of these situations is much more likely when the physician is clear about his or her own role, aware of the limitations of current treatments, and aware of the basis of the patient's hopes and anger.

As a profession, we need to be constantly on the lookout for these difficult areas, these areas where we deal with human suffering and grief that cannot be totally relieved. In these situations, we need to clarify what the clinician can and should do, both to feel useful and to be doing useful things. A failure to do this often causes us to neglect or avoid these very situations. In the past decade, advances have been made in areas such as dealing with the dying patient and the family of the dying patient. We have not prevented death; we have narrowed the gap between our goal and the patient's expectations.

3. Assume That You Are Indispensable to Your Patient and to Your Profession

Now of course, you all know that not one of us is indispensable, but why is it that in spite of knowing, some of you, in fact by your action, deny the need for vacations, weekends off, love, and caring? Why do you insist on always being on the treadmill bearing the anxieties of clinical responsibility for other people's lives day in and day out? Some of you have never established priorities that include not only your patients and profession, but also self, spouse, and family. Why is it that some clinicians never do find time for developing constructive interests outside of medicine and for relating to their families?

We all need to be needed. It is part of humanity. A reasonable need to be needed by our patients may help us to be caring when necessary, say at 3 o'clock on Sunday morning. An excessive need to be needed by patients may cause us to neglect our own needs and those of our families. Medicine becomes a strain when the physician asks himself or herself to give more than he or she has given. The care of other persons rather than one's self is an excellent form of adaptation as long as the self is also cared for. Evidence is mounting that the physician most vulnerable to the stress of practice is the physician from an emotionally barren childhood where feelings of insecurity were frequent (Vaillant & McArthur, 1972). Such feelings carried into adulthood create an excessive need to be liked, appreciated, accepted, needed, and valued. By neglecting to establish personal priorities, some physicians fall into a pattern of having these needs met almost solely by their patients and their profession. The physicians who excessively seek to meet their patients' needs run three risks: the risk of not allowing time for their own dependency needs to be met, the risk of depriving their families' needs for a spouse and parent, and the risk of developing over-dependency in patients. Such a physician may enjoy the dependency of these patients. In fact, the relationship may be such that it is difficult for the doctor to see such a patient either die or get better.

4. Assume Your Personal Quest for Security Will Be Met Through Your Profession Alone

Some students believe that they will feel secure upon obtaining an M.D. Some physicians believe security will arrive upon completing an internship or upon receipt of their Royal College Fellowship. Others expect insecurity to disappear when they have enough patients, enough money, or have obtained the rank of Full Professor. I believe some insecurity is a reality for all of us. Some insecurity may promote professional success. Excessive insecurity results in excessive needs to be liked, appreciated, and valued. Our profession may provide one security blanket, but, at least in Canada, one needs more than one blanket during the cold winter.

5. Assume Professional Esteem and Self-Esteem Are the Same

Self-esteem is influenced by how we evaluate ourselves, by how we think others evaluate and value us. Some doctors live as if the professional esteem obtained from patients, the medical community, and the professional societies, produces high self-esteem. Later, they are dismayed and deflated to find that while they may be held in high esteem in these very demanding and competitive areas, it does not follow that they are automatically loved and esteemed by their spouses and children. Personal esteem from friends and loved ones often is more enduring than professional esteem.

Security and self-esteem are closely related in our daily experience. When we feel secure in our relationships with patients, peers, friends, families, we feel good about ourselves. Threats to our security in any one of these areas in turn threatens our self-esteem. It is therefore hazardous to put all one's eggs in the basket of professional esteem. Physicians who seek security only in financial success and equate self-esteem with financial success run the risk of being wealthy and lonely, or even worse in our unpredictable economy, poor and lonely. (If it could happen to Chrysler, it could happen to you. The government is not likely to subsidize you.) Often the physician who is held in great esteem professionally is the least appreciated by spouse and children and lacks intimate relationships. These personal relationships offer a security and sense of value that are more enduring and less transient than professional acclaim. I believe it is unwise to sacrifice these potentially more enduring relationships for transient appreciation from our profession and peers. We tend to be achievers with strong needs to go on achieving. We should not forget that we also have needs to be cared for, even though we unflatteringly call them "dependency needs." Perhaps, Ingmar Bergman's film "Wild Strawberries" should be made compulsory viewing in every physician's career.

6. Assume Your Emotional Relationship With Patients Is Unimportant and Therefore Need Not Be Examined or Modified

It comes naturally. However, the reality is that some doctors suffer from overidentification with their patients, while the public frequently accuses us of being too cold and too aloof. The doctor's relationship to the patient is influenced by the skills and knowledge the doctor brings to the relationship; it is also influenced by the doctor's feeling relationship to the patient. The doctor is in a relationship with the patient where he or she assumes considerable responsibility at a critical period in the patient's life. The question is where should we be in our emotional relationship with the patient.

This has implications for the teaching of medical students and physicians. As Gorlin and Zucker (1983) recently noted:

> teaching centered entirely on the patient's medical and psychological problems covertly suggests that the doctor's own reactions are trivial or that they should be suppressed or simply mastered. At best, the trainee with strong reactions feels lonely; at worst, he/she may feel guilt, shame, and resentment. When it is made clear that all doctors, however humane, will at times have negative or positive feelings and impulses that can interfere with optimal professional action or judgment, the student is free to consider to a particular patient or a particular disease. Each of us, after all, has special vulnerabilities, usually with unconscious roots; by acknowledging his or her own emotional position, the doctor is able to consider the relationship with the patient more objectively.

In the profession of psychotherapy some training emphasizes the examination of "countertransference" while some types of training does not. Even when emphasized, these feelings are usually examined more with an eye toward impact on the patient and less on the long range implications for the therapist's personal adjustment.

Our emotional tone should lie between identification with the patient, on one extreme, and a cold isolated aloofness, on the other extreme. We call it empathy. To empathize with patients who are seriously ill, we have to appreciate how they think and how they feel without being overcome by our own identification with their situation or without isolating ourselves from them. We are most aware of our feelings when dealing with someone who is like us, someone our age, our nationality, our profession, or our sex. The physician who overidentifies with patients finds himself or herself on an emotional roller-coaster. The doctor who is too aloof does not provide the emotional support, the evidence of appropriate concern, that makes the patient feel valued. It has been said facetiously that every doctor should have gray hair and hemorrhoids—the gray hair in order to look distinguished and the hemorrhoids to produce a look of concern.

To avoid identification or aloofness, we should admit that in the presence of overwhelming disease we often have strong feelings that may include anxiety, guilt, and profound inadequacy. Our training should not be merely technological, but should provide an opportunity for students, residents, and physicians to admit and share their feelings and how these feelings affect them in the doctor-patient relationship. Awareness of our response allows us to modulate our response. I have often heard patients complaining about uncaring, aloof doctors. I have never heard them complain about a doctor shedding a tear with them. Perhaps the occasional tear might not be evidence of overidentification as much as caring about a particular patient and being able and willing to empathize with the patient's situation.

7. Assume That You Can Be a Clinician and Yet Be Interested Only in Pure Science, Not in Ordinary "People-Problems"

Some clinicians do spend a lot of their professional careers being frustrated by patients' personal and family problems and crises. They find it difficult to find a meaningful role dealing with the dying patient, with bereaved relatives, or with the person behind the chronic illness. Other clinicians, interested in more than pure science, find useful, satisfying roles in these areas.

Much of our training is in crisis situations with the acutely ill in centers of high technology. This does not necessarily prepare us for the common problems seen and treated in the office, usually without high technology. Family physicians for the most part deal with ordinary people, with ordinary problems, and perhaps increasingly with chronic problems such as arthritis, diabetes, obesity, and arteriosclerotic disease. In dealing with such patients, it helps if you like people and can take an interest in them and their problems. Osteoarthritis can become boring; people can be interesting.

I believe that this has some implications about who should enter medical school. Perhaps medical school applicants should be given some idea of the problems with which they will deal later on. This would be more accurate than the impressions often generated by medical dramas on television or even the news media reports of new technology and new procedures.

Medicine has many places for pure scientists, such as research, pathology, or radiology. The clinician who is not truly interested in people will find adaptation to clinical practice difficult.

8. Assume Cynicism Could Never Become Your Problem

The above propositions apply only to others, but not to you. You can adapt without consciously establishing your role or worrying about priorities and such soft issues as security, self-esteem, and empathy. Maybe you can, but why do you suppose so many doctors in their forties become cynical? Many are cynical about their profession, about life, and about all those patients with their unreasonable demands for our "free" service. Trapped and choiceless is the way some doctors see their lives. Some are inclined to dismiss this as just part of the mid-life syndrome. You are realizing that you are mortal and starting to go downhill and cynicism is just one defense against despair, but some become much more cynical than others. Medical students have been studied more than physicians. A number of studies have noted that medical students often replace their initial altruism with cynicism as a defense against the anxiety generated by medical training (Bloom, 1965).

I believe cynicism is more common in physicians, who, for a variety of reasons, work themselves into physical and emotional fatigue and exhaustion. They have been overcommitted to work and have not established priorities that permitted and encouraged self-renewal. Self-renewal comes from providing some time for friends, for family, for vacations, for recreation, and indeed some time to do nothing. These experiences allow one the opportunity to regain perspective, humor, patience, emotional and physical strength. The absence of a spiritual view of this life and this world may add to the cynicism. Many physicians do not have a spiritual life that refills them, that assures them of their value as a person, that provides them with a meaning and a philosophy of life that can encompass the suffering they see and share.

Cynicism is frequently recorded as one of the signs of burnout. I believe this often comes about when we expect too much from our work; we expect it to provide not only for our physical and emotional needs, but also for our spiritual needs. Is it not asking too much of our work when we ask it to provide us with life's meaning and purpose and identity? Some physicians seek to find their value, self-esteem and self-worth, their meaning in life, all in their identity as a doctor. In so defining themselves, their self-worth is tied solely to achievement so they become first of all achievers who work in frustrating work, with frustrating patients, frustrating diseases and schedules. The frustration is compounded when the physician who wishes to view himself or herself as an independent professional is increasingly viewed by society as a civil servant dependent upon the public purse. When the sense of achievement is frustrated, self-worth is frustrated especially if work is the sole source of one's sense of self-worth.

This is what I believe the writer of the *Time* magazine essay "The Burnout of Almost Everyone" was getting at in this sentence: "A race of urban nomads, who have wandered far from their family roots tend to turn work into the spiritual hearth, a chief source of warmth and support" (Morrow, 1981, p. 96). I believe that the writer is saying that our work must have a meaning, but when our life has meaning and purpose our work can help us fulfill that meaning and purpose.

9. Assume That No Patient Will Ever Be Angry at You, or Leave Your Practice for Another Doctor

We are social creatures by nature. Most of us have needs to be liked. We need some evidence that what we do is appreciated by someone. To maintain feelings of self-worth and self-esteem, some positive feedback is helpful. We not only need to be aware of the extent to which this is true of us, but we should know that it is inevitable that some patients will be angry at us even if we practice good medicine. Some people's relationships with authority figures are characterized by anger. Some patients will be angry because you have been the one who told them of their incurable disease. Since we are not perfect, sometimes patients will be angry at us because we have made mistakes. Sometimes we make patients angry unnecessarily; the most common reason I hear is "waiting in the doctor's office for two or three hours for a previously scheduled appointment." This often is rightly perceived as disrespect for the patient's own time and schedule.

Some doctors are quite upset when they lose a patient to another doctor. Those with shaky self-esteem are especially threatened. I believe that this experience is most noticeable and therefore most traumatic in small communities. What can one say except, it happens; if you expect it, then you will not be devastated by it.

10. Assume That All Patients Will Be Lovable and Therefore Will Bring Out the Best in You

The perfect doctor, you say, knows all, loves all, and heals all; but, what if someone comes along who blows your perfect doctor image and makes you feel completely helpless, de-skilled, or angry? If we think about it, we can all recall patients whose appointments we enjoy. We also have to admit that we cringe when we see certain names in our appointment book. Sometimes we find ourselves reacting more than understanding. I recall one man with a Cockney accent; his interview always irritated me. At first, I thought it was the accent that turned me off. I later came to realize that it was a combination of his narcissism and my inability to bring about any change in him that made me feel helpless and angry. The poor man is now dead and I am left with an acquired dislike of Cockney accents.

We physicians define the situation as "the difficult patient." I suspect patients have a category of "the difficult doctor." There may be truth in both categorizations. The physician shares with the patient the need to conquer illness, the need to perceive the physician as strong and knowledgeable, the need to deny anxiety about possible death. The patients we classify as "difficult" are those that tend to decrease our self-esteem, provoke guilt or shame in us or rouse unacceptable sexual or aggressive urges. Our need and expectation to be loved and appreciated must be abandoned with the difficult patient.

In a helpful article James Groves (1978) noted that the patients we dread are usually characterized by an insatiable dependency. In turn, he classified these excessively dependent patients into four groups: the dependent clingers, the entitled demanders, the manipulative help rejectors, and the self-destructive deny-ers. He notes that when a physician meets such a patient

> a number of processes may ensue: there may be helplessness in the helper; there may be unconscious punishment of the patient; there may be self-punishment by the doctor; there may be inappropriate confrontation of the patient; and there may be a desperate attempt to avoid or to extrude the patient from the care-giving system.

What can the physician do when confronted with the difficult patient? First of all, we should be comfortable in admitting that some patients do evoke these feelings within us. It is often said physicians tend to intellectualize their problems. Perhaps this is an appropriate response to this problem. We can seek to discover in our own practice what it is about particular patients that make them difficult for us. In the process, we may learn something about patients as well as about ourselves. We may learn how to manage many of these patients, and we may learn that in some situations it is appropriate for us to transfer the patient to someone else, if that is possible. By being aware of our feelings, we can deliberately avoid responses that would be destructive to the patient. Groves (1978) notes

> what the behaviors of such patients teach over time is that it is not how one feels about them that is most important in their care. It is how one behaves towards them: . . . negative feelings about medical and surgical patients constitute important clinical data about the patient's psychology. When the patient creates in a doctor feelings that are disowned or denied, errors in diagnosis and treatment are more likely to occur . . . such disavowal wastes clinical data that may be helpful in treating the "hateful" patient.

A parallel theme has been noted among social workers. Two authors recently noted

> people generally expect a certain amount of appreciation for what they do. However, in addition to not being appreciated, professionals in the social services are often the targets of attacks by clients who resist their efforts to help or do everything they can to thwart them. Consequently, social workers feel guilty for not being more competent. Finally, "involuntary" clients often have recourse to verbal or physical violence, or even written threats, complaints against the worker, and so forth. (Bourgault & Meloche, 1982)

11. Assume Your Marriage and Family Relationships Require Only Your Spare Time and Energy

Many physicians become so involved in their professional lives that inadvertently the families only receive the time and energy that is left over. Yet, an enduring, intimate relationship with one's spouse, in a relationship that involves the mutual meeting of needs, can be one important source of having one's dependency and security needs met. Such a relationship also sustains self-esteem. Children grow up. The physician who has a close warm relationship with his or her adult children is to be envied.

These relationships don't just happen. They come about because they were important to the physician from the beginning. Further, such physicians have usually arranged their priorities so that they made time for their spouse and children regularly throughout the years. The problem is that this requires time together, to learn the needs of our partners, for only then can love be communicated to our spouses in a way that meets their needs. We have to learn to communicate love to our spouses in a manner that is understood as being love by them; in this, each marriage is unique.

But, time is precisely what the doctor complains he or she lacks. However, if I am correct, with the physician's changing role and status, there will be less grandiose admiration of physicians outside the home. The doctor may well need his or her home even more in the future than he or she has in the past; therefore, the doctor must make time. Many physicians start out with the good intentions of spending time with their families, but each activity planned is a "routine family matter." Repeatedly, the routine gets pushed out by the urgent problems that come up in the medical practice. After many years of marriage, the physician looks back to see that the urgencies of practice have always replaced the routines of the marriage and the family, until suddenly the whole family life is either an emergency or a catastrophe.

This may be resolved by saying that there are certain times that practice is first and certain other times that spouse and family are first. Then, life must be arranged accordingly. If we do not take this step, our families get squeezed out of our lives by the things in our lives that are either scheduled or are emergencies. Therefore, we must schedule our spouse and families into our lives. The physician must realize his or her importance to the spouse and family and their importance to the physician's own well-being.

12. The Male Physician Should Assume That He Is God's Gift to Women, and Tell His Wife That Her Feelings of Jealousy Are All Based on Her Low-Esteem and That's Her Fault.

Some patients fall in love with their doctor. The scenario often goes something like this. The patient is a young lady with a tumor or with a minor illness and is unhappily married or is divorced. She comes to her physician not only with her specific complaints, but at a time when she is feeling frightened and helpless. In his office, the doctor seems strong, confident, calm, and caring. He knows what to do and does it. He helps her with her presenting problem. She then is relieved and gains strength from his confidence. She begins to think, "Isn't he wonderful, he'd be so nice to have around the house." Meanwhile, back in the doctor's home, his wife is also thinking, "he'd be so nice to have around the house" or less kindly, "if patients could only see him like I do."

Next our patient communicates to the doctor that he's wonderful. He immediately agrees and, after careful thought, concludes that she is a genius and wishes his wife was smart this way also. He says to himself "excellent judge of men, that girl."

The problem is he mistakes her needs for his assets. Typically, the situation involves two people with unmet needs. The physician at risk is one whose needs to be cared for are not being met at home. Sometimes this has been due to his busyness, sometimes because he denied any such need. Often, his wife is tired of giving of herself with little apparent attempt by her husband to meet her various needs as a husband and father of her children. She is now putting demands on her husband to do something at home. She is tired of feeling she is nothing but his housekeeper and sexual partner. He often responds to these demands by feeling unappreciated and nothing but a breadwinner. At such a time, he is a sitting duck for a relationship with a young lady with needs that also make her vulnerable. The affair at first not only boosts sagging self-esteem for both, but seems to offer the doctor a relationship in which he may receive much more admiration than he gets at home with much less responsibility. She, who has no right to this man, can be warm and accepting at first. Meanwhile, his wife, who feels she has a right to him, is becoming more angry and frustrated about his increasing absence from the home. Later, the young lady begins to feel she has some rights too. She then begins to demand some responsibility and she begins to make requests that increasingly sound like demands; she begins to feel jealous. Now our emotionally depleted doctor feels he has two demanding women and still no one to look after him.

How may such a predicament be prevented? First, realize it happens, and it starts primarily because of the role of the two people in the situation. Realize it begins because of her needs, not your assets. Realize that when you meet dependent needs with an erotic response, you become part of the problem, not part of the solution. The best prevention is to be sure that your own needs to be cared for (dependent needs) are being met. These are best met in a marriage where there is a reciprocity of mutual need-meeting. Perhaps the early warning signal is when you begin to feel that your patients appreciate you and love you more than your wife and family do. The next step may be to spend even more time with patients and less with your spouse.

13. Women Physicians Assume That Being a Physician Is Easy

Women physicians don't have to worry about the issues discussed above, but simply have to be super doctors, super wives, and super moms. As a judge might say, the sentences are served concurrently.

The truth, of course, is that a female physician can have the same stress as a male physician, but she may have additional stress. In a traditionally male profession, she not only has to prove herself, but may feel that she represents females and cannot let her sex down. Many are wives and mothers who carry a heavier responsibility in the home than most male physicians. In our survey of Ontario female physicians in 1974 (Tatham, Hill, & Vincent, 1976), we found 1,617 female physicians. In our random sample of 200, 50% were working over 40 hours per week and 75% were working more than 20 hours per week in medicine. Slightly over 64% were married and combining roles of wife and physician (Vincent et al., 1976). About half were married to male physicians. Sixty percent of our sample felt that being a woman in medicine presented them with greater stress in certain areas than other women. The most common difficulties mentioned were: conflict between home and career, long irregular hours and fatigue, limited social and recreational time, greater responsibilities and difficult social relations in nonmedical groups. Combining profession and marriage proved more difficult than anticipated for 52.5% of respondents. The typical dilemma was summed up by one of our respondents as follows: "If I devote as much time to practice, professional organizations, and education as I should, I feel my family suffers. If I devote the time I would like to give my family, then society resents my not using my training more of the time." Nevertheless, the great majority of them gave evidence that both profession and marriage were much enjoyed. A frequent need expressed was for better domestic help. The emotional problems of running a home and practice seemed far less conflicting than the mechanics of the combination.

Major obstacles to resolving the conflicting priorities were lack of part-time employment opportunities and, particularly, lack of flexibility in internship and residency programs. These programs have been arranged in an all or nothing fashion, which have been satisfactory for most male physicians. Many young women appear to wish to combine the early years of child-rearing with post-graduate training. This has been shown to be possible. However, it is impossible with inflexible residency programs that do not allow opportunity for part-time training of longer duration than the standard full-time program. "Biology is destiny" is not as true about male-female roles as was once thought. However, pregnancy does differentiate women from men. The care of a child can be divided with the husband, but the bearing of the child is the woman's experience alone. Women in medicine should not have to ask for special consideration for this fact; rather, the medical system should take this difference into consideration. This means the building of more flexible programs of training and practice opportunities to allow for both part-time training and work. Also, the means of re-entry for women physicians, who have discontinued practice for a few years must be made more available.

It is virtually impossible to be a full-time homemaker for husband and children and, at the same time, have a full-time, demanding profession. Other things being equal, time must be taken from one role to fill the other role. In our survey, women physicians complained frequently about the lack of adequate household help. Rarely did they complain about the lack of household help from their husbands. One might assume that physicians' husbands do much more around the house than do other husbands. Our data did not confirm this for the majority. While family planning, more day care centers, and better domestic help are all beneficial for a woman who wishes to combine medicine with a family, nothing else will be as important to her success in this combination as the attitude of her husband. A young man who marries a physician should not think of his wife as having two jobs, a profession and a home, while he has one job. The divide should be more equitable and will vary with the individual couple and the phase of the family cycle. Men marrying physicians should be prepared to become intimately involved within the family and home, which has traditionally been the woman's domain. Each helps the other. The man gives up some of his career opportunities and load, but gains some of woman's traditional satisfactions in the home, especially in relations with one's growing and grown children. A male who can do this must be strong enough in his own identity so that it is shattered neither by doing dishes nor having a wife successful in her career.

14. Assume Nothing in Our Society Has Changed Since We Were Kids

This might require us to believe the following: women's roles and self-perceptions have not really changed. The public is aware that physicians are reliable and trustworthy authority figures, who make no mistakes and accept poverty without ever having taken the vow. Patients don't really want to know what is wrong with them and don't expect any explanations as to what we are doing and why.

We all feel that these statements are not really true. The doctor-patient relationship seems to be changing for a variety of reasons. The patients have changed over the years. They are more educated in general and more knowledgeable about medicine in particular. Many have been influenced by the consumerism movement throughout society, so we hear complaints about physicians being too rushed or too impersonal. The current generation seems to have more faith in science and technology than in people; thus, while they have greater faith in scientific medicine, they seem to have less faith in physicians. Patients are now more likely than in the recent past to harbour both anti-establishment and egalitarian values.

An Ohio study recently confirmed some of these impressions (Haug & Lavin, 1979). The authors concluded that their survey had shown the existence of widespread challenges to the authority of physicians, a phenomenon previously recorded only impressionistically by the media. This attitude characterized more than half of their sample. Variables related to this attitude were: a younger age, a higher educational level, and greater health knowledge often associated with a consumerist orientation. These people often questioned the physicians' concern for people. The authors felt their study confirmed that norms of patient trust, confidence, and obedience are being eroded. They concluded

> thus, physicians concerned with the future of physician-patient relationships will note the implication emerging from this study that overall decline and acceptance of authority and trust in people has not left the medical profession untouched . . . Given that these challenge trends are not likely to fade away, physicians will have to find ways of dealing with behavioral challenge, the form of phenomena of most direct relevance to physician-patient relationships. Those in primary care are already, in many cases, adopting a co-operative or even a bargaining relationship with patients, and this may well become the mode of the future for this level of care. (Haug & Lavin, 1979)

Perhaps some of these societal trends are part of the ethos of those now graduating in medicine. An attitudinal study conducted on physicians in Detroit recently indicated that women were generally more liberal and egalitarian than men, but that the younger male physicians were considerably more liberal and egalitarian than older male physicians (Heins et al., 1979).

Another recent Ohio study (Mawardi, 1979) of stresses in medical practice showed some new stresses not found in earlier studies. These included the growing number of malpractice suits and the practicing of defensive medicine. Another new stress that very clearly reflects on the doctor-patient relationship was that a number of physicians expressed fear of violence against themselves and their families by disgruntled patients.

Many other changes are at work that influence the doctor-patient relationship, such as the increasing role of government and community in the organization of medical practice, the team approach, and the increasing assertiveness of paramedical groups. We will continue to be faced with difficult ethical decisions around the question of the value of human life. These will influence decisions about abortion, euthanasia, and the distribution of limited resources for patient care.

CONCLUSION

The operation of the above fourteen assumptions has not been proven by rigorous experimentation or research. Indeed, it is extremely difficult to either prove or disprove many of the points because of the problem in isolating these factors for research. They have, however, comprised trends I have observed in my clinical practice when physicians were patients. I offer them to the reader not as dogmatic statements, but as food for thought. Given the multitude of hazards that psychiatrists, social workers, and psychologists face, it is my impression that the vast majority adapt remarkably well to their chosen profession. It is clear that a studied consideration of these hazardous assumptions should help avoid the therapist becoming the casualty.

REFERENCES

A'Brook, M. F., Hailstone, J. D., & McLauchlan, I. E. J. Psychiatric illness in the medical profession. *British Journal of Psychiatry,* 1967, *113,* 1013-1023.

Bloom, S. W. The sociology of medical education: Some comments on the state of a field, *Milbank Memorial Fund Quarterly,* April 1965, *43* (#2, part I), 143-184.

Bourgault, D., & Meloche, M. Burnout or dying of exhaustion like a chameleon on a kilt. *Social Worker Le Travailleur Social,* 1982, *50,* #3.

Gorlin R., & Zucker, H. Physicians' reactions to patients. *New England Journal of Medicine,* 1983, *308,* 1059-1063.

Groves, J. E. Taking care of the hateful patient. *New England Journal of Medicine,* 1978, *298,* 883-887.

Haug, M. R., & Lavin, B. Public challenge of physician authority. *Medical Care,* 1979, *17,* 844-858.

Heins, M., et al. Attitudes of women and men physicians. *American Journal of Public Health,* 1979, *69,* 1132-1139.

Mawardi, B. H. Satisfactions, dissatisfactions, and causes of stress in medical practice. *Journal of the American Medical Association,* 1979, *241,* #14.

Morrow, L. The burnout of almost everyone. *Time Magazine,* April 15, 1981, p. 96.

Murray, R. M. Psychiatric illness in doctors. *Lancet,* 1974, *1,* 1211-1213.

Sakinofsky, I. Suicide in doctors and wives of doctors. *Canadian Family Physician,* 1980, *26,* 837-844.

Tatham, M. R., Hill, M. M., & Vincent, M. O. Women physicians in Ontario. *Ontario Medical Review,* July 1976, 342-346.

Vaillant, G. E., Brighton, J. R., & McArthur, C. Physician's use of mood-altering drugs: A twenty year follow up report. *New England Journal of Medicine,* 1970, *282,* 365-370.

Vaillant, G. E., & McArthur, C. Some psychological vulnerabilities of physicians. *New England Journal of Medicine,* 1972, *287,* 372-375.

Vincent, M. O. The impaired physician and you. *Canadian Family Physician,* 1980, *26,* 861-864.

Vincent, M. O. Mission impossible? *Le Medic du Quebec,* 1973, *8,* 813.

Vincent, M. O., Hill, M. M., & Tatham, M. R. The physician's marriage, husband, family and practice. *Ontario Medical Review,* July 1976, 342-346.

Vincent, M. O., Robinson, E. A., & Latt, L. Physicians as patients: Private psychiatric hospital experience. *Canadian Medical Association Journal,* 1969, *100,* 403-412.

Status: Force and Counterforce

Tom H. Peake
Robert P. Archer

> My art was a philosophy of teaching the sweetness of adversity.
>
> —Charlie Chaplin

When we were graduate students hungry to learn the secrets of psychotherapy, our professors had the audacity to require that we take "core" courses like Social Psychology, Learning Theory, and Statistics. How could real-world clinical secrets be wrapped in these seemingly unrelated academic and esoteric trappings? Fortunately we have found that many were, although it took subsequent dilemmas to reveal their relevance. The purpose of this chapter is to discuss some of the specific relevance and impact we have found from the experimental literature in psychology in terms of the utility of these findings within the context of the practice of clinical psychotherapy.

Specifically, we would like to focus on the clinical implications of research findings concerning *idiosyncracy credit, cognitive dissonance* and *credibility induction.* The data we will refer to derives principally from experimental research, but speaks to vital issues of the context surrounding the practice of therapy, a topic which is rarely addressed directly in the research and writings on psychotherapy training and process. Our position is that these variables exercise both direct and indirect effects on the practice and outcome of psychotherapy. Further, it is suggested that the impact of these concepts may serve to the advantage or disadvantage of the psychotherapists, that is, they may function as two-edged swords. Finally, it is suggested that careful consideration of these variables enables the psychotherapist to use the impact and influence of status in a manner most productive to the psychotherapeutic enterprise.

IDIOSYNCRACY CREDIT

A vivid example of the relevance of experimental data to clinical issues is represented in a series of social psychology studies that Wiggins and his associates (1965) and Hollander (1958, 1960) conducted on the effects of status liability and status use within social or group situations. Since the psychotherapist rarely functions outside of some administrative, peer, or organizational context or group, these studies have direct relevance to the practicing psychotherapist. For example, during the training of the psychotherapist, the resident or intern will invariably function within a context which will require him or her to function as a member of interdisciplinary treatment team. That team is embedded within a larger organizational structure composed of the hospital, clinic, or counseling center. In the practicum or residency training setting, the way a therapist enters the system functions as a crucial, albeit indirect, influence on the effectiveness of that individual in the therapist role.

We will not attempt to cite all of the relevant experimental data that comprise the literature on "status" relevant issues, but rather we will summarize the concept of idiosyncracy credit and its relevance to the variable of status. In a representative study, Hollander (1960) examined the individual's ability to influence other group members in relationship to that person's success in solving (competence) a group task and that person's degree of conformity or nonconformity to group norms. The experimental data were collected from groups engaged in problem solving tasks under controlled conditions. Within each group of five individuals, a confederate evidenced a high degree of competence during a series of 15 group problem solving task trials. The independent variable manipulated by the experimenters consisted of the stage at which the confederate displayed nonconformity to the procedural norms agreed upon by the group, i.e., early, middle, or late in the sequence of problem solving trials. The dependent measure in these studies consisted of the number of trials in which the confederate's recommended solution was accepted as the group's choice. A general main effect was found for the variable of competence. The group was more likely to accept the confederate's solution as the number of trials progressed. This finding indicated that the confederate's influence increased with repeated evidence of his or her competence. Of greater interest was a finding that "past conformity" of the confederate was also found to effect acceptance by group peers. Specifically, the later the individual demonstrated nonconformity to procedural norms, the greater the overall influence of the confederate in determining and influencing the group solutions. Reflecting on the dynamics of these findings, Hollander (1960) stated,

> a person who exhibits both competence and conformity should eventually reach a threshold at which it becomes appropriate in the eyes of others for him to assert influence; and insofar as these assertions are accepted he emerges as a leader . . . status is conceived as an accumulation of positively disposed impressions termed "idiosyncracy credits." A person gains credits . . . by showing competence *and* by conforming to the expectancies applicable to him at the time. Eventually his credits allow him to nonconform with greater impunity. (p. 365)

Thus, Hollander has shown that the influence of an individual who did not conform early in the group process was more dramatically opposed or resisted than that of an equally competent individual who waited to display nonconformity or show some divergent style or technique.

The novice therapist who is oblivious to these principles may often find himself or herself short on group influence in several ways. Status within the field of psychotherapy organizations and groups is frequently related to decisions such as patient assignment, degree and severity of supervisory scrutiny, degree of access and impact on policy-making decisions, and may indirectly influence expectations and reputations concerning therapeutic potency. In our experience, there have been many instances in which trainees' insensitivity to these issues have caused substantial interpersonal struggles that have served to side-track their growth as competent psychotherapists. In this regard, many residents and interns have mistakenly approached their organizations based upon the premise that their competence alone should be sufficient to warrant significant influence within the agency. Stated differently, their assumptions have rested on the premise that "being right was enough." When their well-intentioned advice and suggestions have been met with resistance and disinterest on the part of veteran staff members, they have frequently responded with anger and frustration. The social psychology findings concerning idiosyncracy credit strongly suggest that beyond the issue of competence, the therapist entering an agency, a new community, or a new organizational structure should closely attend to identifying and, at least initially, conforming to well-established group norms and procedures before trying to change prevailing currents within their social setting. At a minimum, these findings suggest that social influence is a multidetermined phenomenon which is only partially accounted for by the individual's competence and performance.

Having discussed one of the variables that impacts a psychotherapist's effectiveness within his or her social milieu, we shall discuss two concepts which have direct relevance for the psychotherapist's impact with clients or patients.

COGNITIVE DISSONANCE

One concept that has significance in terms of facilitating psychotherapeutic effectiveness is *cognitive dissonance.* Cognitive dissonance has been one of the most widely researched and discussed phenomena within the field of social psychology over the past two decades. We will not attempt to review this literature in detail, but rather to summarize the principal concept. Cognitive dissonance refers to situations in which there is a disparity between one's belief or attitude (about some issue) and one's actions or behaviors. Cognitive dissonance theory holds that this discrepancy causes a tension state, or dissonance, which motivates or elicits a desire for consistency, i.e., a need to restore the balance between our beliefs and our actions (or new experiences). Cognitive dissonance theory predicts, for example, that a commitment by actions, including such things as an arduous initiation into a club or organization, or a financial or time investment in a cause or social movement (e.g., religious or political), increases the probability that one will become a strong believer in the rationale of that endeavor. The reader unfamiliar with this concept may wish to read further in Festinger (1957).

The vast majority of psychotherapist orientations require the patient to make substantial investments of both money and time into the therapeutic enterprise to a degree that can create dissonance between these investments and any belief that psychotherapy is not valuable or effective. As the patient continues to invest more and more resources into their psychotherapy treatment, it increasingly becomes probable that the patient will continue to modify his or her beliefs toward a conviction that psychotherapy is a valuable undertaking. In this regard, psychoanalytic treatment has historically served as a striking example of a treatment modality requiring a substantial and prolonged investment of time and money as a basic prerequisite for the change process to occur. Conversely, the briefer forms of psychotherapy including time-limited interventions may be resisted by the patient because of the dissonance created in engaging in such modalities while maintaining a belief that psychotherapy requires a long duration in order to be effective.

Most psychology-trained psychotherapists know the principal of cognitive dissonance, but perhaps too infrequently apply it. During the psychologist's practicum and internship placement experiences, it is frequent for both the institution as well as the trainee to provide substantial reductions or completely eliminate standard psychotherapy fees and to be overly flexible in scheduling appointment hours. While such actions are usually taken as a reflection of the humanistic concerns of the institution and trainee, they are also a reflection of the insecurity and feelings of inadequacy manifested by the trainee in terms of their competence to deliver mental health services. A question infrequently addressed concerning such practices centers upon how a patient is to perceive psychotherapy which comes "too easy and too cheap." Attempting to explain this issue to us, one of our supervisors described the fee setting process in psychotherapy as being similar to "pricing whiskey." If too low a fee is set relative to the individual's (patient's) resources, then the product is seen as being cheap and its value is derogated. A reasonably expensive investment (that may be conceived of in terms of both time and emotional effort in addition to financial investment) sets an expectation that the product or process is of established value and proven quality. The direct implication for the provider of mental health services is that if we wish the patient to expect positive changes from the psychotherapy and to value that process, it requires us to act in a manner which conveys that we value the process and seriously undertake it. For the novice psychotherapist who is prepared to be flexible (to a fault) in terms of scheduling appointments and reducing payment for his or her efforts, the consistent message to the client is that the psychotherapy process is "worthless."

CREDIBILITY INDUCTION

Another concept which is directly related to the creation of conditions that facilitate the psychotherapeutic process is the concept of *credibility induction.* Recently, a related phenomenon has been described by Wickramasekera (in press). He has taken the position that what is commonly referred to as the "placebo effect" is a specifiable variable that may be systematically manipulated by the therapist to increase psychotherapeutic effectiveness. Wickramasekera argues that the mechanism of the placebo effect is classical conditioning in which a conditioned stimulus (placebo stimulus) is paired with an unconditioned stimulus already capable of producing a therapeutic effect or unconditioned response. Thus, for example, the paired presentation of a powerful anti-anxiety psychoactive medication (UCS) with specific setting stimuli such as the therapist's presence (CS) will lead to the capacity of therapist's presence to reduce anxiety in the patient (CR). Further, the placebo phenomena is enhanced by the degree to which such conditioning is able to bypass the influence of the dominant hemisphere functions which include linear and analytic thinking. Like good hypnotic subjects, good placebo responders are seen as those individuals who are able to inhibit the critical-analytic mode of information processing characteristic of the dominant verbal hemisphere, and individuals who are prone to seek conceptual or other relationships between events that seem unrelated to other individuals.

Credibility induction, then, is the ability to systematically mobilize, facilitate, and amplify positive expectations about the effectiveness of psychotherapy by manipulation of the parameters of placebo-related variables. Such variables include the qualities of the caregiver, the characteristics of the situation, and the trappings of the therapeutic interchange. Thus, the concept of credibility induction rests upon a complex view of psychotherapy expectations based upon prior life experience (or conditioning history). These expectations are subject to changes over time and to systematic manipulation. Such a view also clearly suggests that a primary function of the psychotherapist is to carefully evaluate the pre-existing life experience of the patient (which yield their expectations) as he or she enters the psychotherapeutic experience. For the patient who views the practice of medicine as highly effective and powerful, psychotherapy effectiveness may be enhanced by the use of the title "doctor" and the presentation of the trappings of modern medicine as manifested by white laboratory coats and modern biofeedback equipment. Given these patient perceptions, psychologists who wish to continually emphasize to the patient that the practice of psychology is not a subdiscipline of medicine may be meeting their own needs at the expense of those of their patients.

Taken together, the concepts of cognitive dissonance and of credibility induction clearly indicate that the psychotherapist must take careful assessment of the contextual stimuli present within the psychotherapy situation. These contextual stimuli serve to facilitate or interfere with positive psychotherapy outcomes. This is not to suggest that a positive psychotherapy outcome is exclusively or even predominantly the product of such attitude and expectancy variables, but it underscores the fact that psychotherapy is a tremendously complex and delicate task that may often "need all the help it can get." The psychotherapist who ignores the impact of the contextual stimuli and expectancies embedded within his or her psychotherapeutic efforts may do so at the expense of effectively aiding his/her patients.

THE PERSPECTIVE ON STATUS AND INFLUENCE

The effective psychotherapist must frequently strike a delicate and often paradoxical balance between art and science and between illusion and reality in attempting to deliver services to patients. A lyrical and detailed portrait of this balance is provided by Kopp's (1972) description of the sublety of the therapist role. The title of this book, *If You Meet the Buddha on the Road, Kill Him* suggests that the patient both seeks and desires, as well as rejects and fears, a powerful and mysterious figure capable of easing personal suffering. This archetypal need to reach salvation through the efforts of a holy man or powerful other creates a transference issue in psychotherapy which can be utilized to aid in the psychotherapeutic process. If this perception is carelessly or excessively utilized by the psychotherapist, however, it can be most destructive to the psychotherapy process. These dangers are worse if the therapist comes to believe the myth of his or her own importance or power, or if the therapist does not aid the patient to eventually realize the limits of the myth. Several examples from the literature on group processes may be used to illustrate this delicate process.

In terms of group therapy, Bion (1958) and Rioch (1976) have discussed the role of implicit or unconscious group assumptions that served to interfere with the work of a group or organization. They suggest that there are three types of unconscious fantasies about leadership which tend to emerge within group processes to interfere with the conscious work of the group. These fantasies consist of the following: (a) themes of dependence and independence; (b) themes of fight and flight, and/or (c) a theme of pairing that may occur between the group leader and a member of the group that, within the context of the group myth, will produce a messiah capable of great achievements and tremendous power. These processes operate as a type of group transference to the leader. The leader of the group can attempt to accommodate and complement these early unconscious wishes. For example, the leader may attempt to meet the need for protection and dependence by providing the group with assurance concerning their omnipotence. The power and status that this contract between leader and group provides is short-lived. It rapidly becomes clear that the leader is not capable of delivering the group members from all difficulties and harms. To the extent that the group leader actually believes the group myth, his or her status will be fleeting and destructive to the group's natural development and growth, a danger referred to by the Greeks as *hubris.* Bion has suggested that the most constructive and effective use of power and leadership entails recognizing the basic group myths and assumptions directed towards the leader and mobilizing these forces as a constructive influence without falling prey to their seductive or provocative potential. Eventually, leadership power can be used to reveal to the group the influence of the unconscious perceptions and processes.

CONCLUSION

In conclusion, this chapter has extended findings from basic social and clinical research to the psychotherapeutic process. While these types of extrapolations are tenuous, they offer guidance to the novice psychotherapist concerning ways of entering the mental health agency, agency subgroups, and the clinical psychotherapy context. The explicit consideration of such issues as status and expectancies serves to increase both the therapist's clinical and organizational effectiveness.

REFERENCES

Bion, W. R. *Experiences in groups.* New York: Dover, 1958.

Festinger, L. *A theory of cognitive dissonance.* New York: Row, Peterson, 1957.

Hollander, E. P. Conformity, status, and idiosyncracy credit. *Psychological Review.* 1958, *65,* 117-127.

Hollander, E. P. Competence and conformity in the acceptance of influence. *Journal of Abnormal and Social Psychology.* 1960, *61,* 365-369.

Kopp, S. *If you meet the Buddha on the road, kill him!: The Pilgrimage of psychotherapy patients.* Ben Lomond, California: Science & Behavior Books, 1972.

Rioch, M. J. "The Work of Wilfred Bion on Groups" in Kissen, M. (Ed.) *From Group dynamics to group psychoanalysis.* New York: Wiley, 1976.

Wickramasekera, I. A conditioned response model of the placebo effect: Predictions from the model. In L. White et al. (Eds.), *Placebo: clinical phenomena and new insights.* New York: Guilford, in press.

Wiggins, J. A., Dill, F., and Schwartz, R. D. On status-liability. *Sociometry,* 1965, *28,* 197-209.

THE SYSTEMS OF TRAINING: PAST, PRESENT AND FUTURE ISSUES

A Profile of Training in Clinical Psychology

James M. Anker

INTRODUCTION

After thirty-six years as a student of psychology, and only slightly less than that as a professional and a "trainer," I must admit to a degree of confusion and disappointment with the art of preparing professionals I see in my field. Having served on clinical faculties, as Director of a Ph.D. program in clinical psychology, as an APA site visitor, and as an examiner for the American Board of Professional Psychology, it seems to me that over these years we could have done better.

Not that we have done so badly, perhaps, nor have we had all that long to do it in. My own career spans the time over which clinical psychology was born, or at least was being weaned, in its present state to development. So, hopefully without appearing to be too critical, there may be value in taking a look from a distance at several areas of importance in professional training.

HISTORY

In 1946, the Veterans Administration began the training program in clinical psychology under the direction of James G. Miller, M.D., Ph.D. The Veterans Administration, feeling the press of a large number of post-World War II veterans in its hospitals and clinics, and only recently aware of the potential value of psychologists trained as clinicians, began this pioneering program which started a movement in clinical psychology training and has continued to this day. The profession owes the Veterans Administration, past and present, a resounding thanks for probably the most substantial contributions to clinical training in the field. Prior to World War II, psychologists, even those who may have had some clinical interests, typically were exposed only to intelligence testing and perhaps work with mental retardation. The violent social forces of the War and the great need for qualified personnel, as well as a latent interest in psychology to develop more in clinical directions, eventuated in the sudden emergence of the possibility of psychology as a clinical profession.

The VA program formalized supervised clinical experience for "trainees" who were provided stipends during their training. Qualified supervisors and consultants were identified with the program and training became a bona fide part of the duty assignment of many VA psychologists. A close relationship was begun between the VA, centrally and in the field, and universities providing academic preparation. The budgetary justification for the program was to provide a pool of qualified clinical psychologists from which the VA could recruit ever-increasing numbers of staff. They were successful in meeting this objective and, in doing so, provided clinical experience and training to many clinical psychologists who largely were to set the course for the profession.

In 1947, David Shakow, first chairing a committee, and then through the discussions and resolutions of the Boulder Conference on Training in Clinical Psychology, developed an educational format which came into wide use and acceptance for the training of professional clinical psychologists, the scientist-professional or "Boulder" model. There was a strong emphasis on ensuring proper and controlled clinical experience, something which psychologists, unlike their medical counterparts, had not formerly had. Shakow's model also outlined a pattern of academic preparation appropriate to the preparation of the scientist-professional. Shakow stressed, although I believe it was not attended to properly, that the patterns of clinical training and curricula presented in the report were offered as *models,* and that the objective of supervision and academic experience should not be to deliver a finished practitioner, but rather to develop a base which would enable a student to continue to learn, develop, stay up with the field, and offer the best and most responsible service.

Since the time of the Boulder Conference, there have been additional conferences on training in clinical psychology, all of which returned to address the perennial question of the balance between the scientist and the professional. At the Vail Conference the issue was focused more sharply by looking at the role of the scientist in relation to the *practitioner.* More recently, we have seen the development of the Psy.D. degree designed to change the emphasis from research training to professional or practitioner training. Schools of professional psychology have been established in which the Ph.D. or Psy.D. degrees, or both, are offered. We have gone though a period of change which in some respects is revolutionary. And yet, it seems that basic questions and problems with which we have been struggling for almost the last two score years largely have not been resolved in a wholly satisfactory and lasting fashion.

CURRICULUM

Recent concern arose that many applied programs, particularly those in clinical psychology (both Ph.D. and Psy.D.), were not providing enough "basic science" psychology. Changes in accreditation standards and the move toward certification of psychology departments caused universities offering clinical training programs to readdress the need for basic or core knowledge in the discipline of psychology upon which to base the development of able professionals. The response, in many cases, has begun to develop a roster of required courses, sometimes to the extent that much of "doctoral" level training is occupied by such prescription. Additionally, clinical programs, in the same prescriptive fashion, typically require those courses which are "necessary" for the practicing professional. These include courses dealing with cultural diversity, psychotherapy, psychopathology, personality assessment, professional practice and ethics, psychopharmacology, and neuropsychology, among others. These of course are in addition to the basic science courses and courses in statistics and experimental design.

In totalling these courses, I am impressed and dismayed by the relative lack of flexibility that such requirements, which I see as excessive, produce. If we are to maintain the essence of preparing

Ph.D.s, as opposed to practitioners alone, we must recognize the importance of highly tailored scholarly work at the doctoral level. At the same time, the forces for conforming to credentialing and certification of programs are such that there is an intrinsic and perhaps unavoidable conflict in which departments, faculty, and students must be embroiled.

I don't know the answer. Perhaps there is none. More likely there are many. However, I am convinced that the answer is not simply to develop a roll call of all currently relevant courses in the field and to require, or virtually require, all Ph.D. or Psy.D. students to take them. This movement has resulted in what appears to be a serious diminution of the role of the doctoral committee in the preparation of Ph.D. students, and a *pro forma* approach to clinical supervision at advanced levels in assessment and intervention.

Shakow, in his 1947 Committee on Training in Clinical Psychology report, referenced Flexner's "Medical Education" written in 1925. Like Flexner, he emphasized that the goal of professional training was not to provide the specific procedures and knowledge available in the field at the time and to ensure that all students were able to learn and master them. He recognized that many of these procedures and concepts would quickly be outdated. Students who had no alternatives would be left well behind their times. The thrust was to develop a program of professional learning which would carry the students-turned-professional adaptably through to the end of their careers. I am concerned that we may be falling back on prescription instead of upon the development of patterns of mature professional learning.

FACULTY

Over the years I have heard students testifying to the wonders, or lack thereof, of experiences in clinical supervision. I haven't kept data. Probably most students would favor supervision by nonfaculty, people who do "real" clinical work. There may be some validity to that observation. After all, most Ph.D. clinicians who become faculty members do not do so because they are primarily interested in clinical occupations. If they were, they likely would go into the public or private practice of clinical psychology. I suppose we tend to be somewhat more eggheaded, interested in research, and/or attracted to the more didactic activities of the teacher than to our practicing brethren. Hence some faculty entrusted with the fundamental training of clinical psychologists may not have much interest or skill in clinical occupations themselves. Even if they do, it is not unlikely that they themselves will have received little or no preparation in the skills of supervising psychotherapy or other clinical activities.

The interest of faculty in clinical activities, as well as their interest in clinical supervision, obviously varies greatly. It is unlikely, however, that any good clinical program can maintain itself at a level of quality, academically or clinically, without a serious and dedicated faculty oriented toward the clinical as well as the academic aspects of the profession. In departments where faculty have not had a clear commitment to the "clinical side," it is my view that morale among students has been poor and achievements following graduation were based all too much on the individual merits of the students and relatively little upon the excellence of their preparation. In departments lacking in academic or scholarly commitment students have appeared to me to present an unconvincing and shallow over-evaluation of the "tools of the trade" and leave the university more as time-bound tradesmen than as creative professionals.

There is another problem for faculty interested in clinical supervision. Faculty assignment patterns and reward systems in universities typically are such so that these activities may not be recognized properly as "load" and may not weigh significantly in promotion, tenure, and salary increases. There is, in many departments I believe, a real question of whether or not supervision of clinical work is credited at all, although most say that it is.

Finally, one must seriously consider the effects of modeling on students as they progress through traditional doctoral programs. Most academicians would like to present students with an appropriate array of models, clinical and academic, to allow them a reasonable opportunity to sense the depth and breadth of the field and, having done so, to permit them to make a reasonable choice about personal and professional objectives. It appears that faculty modeling may not be terribly good in many cases. Clinical work done by faculty in private practices, which might be excellent, is almost always done in the absence of students. As a matter of fact, in some cases it has been suggested that faculty who had private practices became so engrossed in them, and perhaps in the opportunity to make additional income, that they slighted the supervision of students and the preparation of their courses. In any case clinical Ph.D.

programs and Psy.D. programs have a significant issue to face in the proper modeling of skills and value for their students, in both the clinical and scholarly arenas.

CLINICAL EXPERIENCE AND SUPERVISION

It has been standard policy, established for good reason I believe, for students in clinical training programs to begin clinical activities early in their careers rather than taking academic material first and then getting an internship and other supervisory experience. The wisdom, I believe, is compelling. The development of clinical skills requires a relatively prolonged exposure to clinical problems in appropriate professional settings with an opportunity for close interaction with a "supervisor" from whom the student may learn some of the conventional wisdom, prudence and most importantly, the decision-making processes which are the basic measure of professional excellence. I fear, however, that too much of clinical training and clinical supervision emphasizes procedures; the detection of clues or observations which permits a "correct" DSM-III diagnosis, just exactly what is unconditional positive regard, how to deal with a schizophrenic, etc. Such information and knowledge, which I believe are necessary in the preparation of a professional clinician, are not sufficient. I, and many of my colleagues, expect our professionals to have a wide and deep knowledge of their field in terms of the basic sciences, the current literature, procedures and concepts, and all matters directly related to the proper practice and improvement of the profession and its services. However, in working with an individual patient, to *focus* upon the diagnosis, or the "right" way to pursue treatment, or whether or not this procedure is correct or not, is pedestrian and likely to ill-equip a student entering the profession. Rather, it is compelling to me to consider the whole panoply of information that a patient and his or her context provides. Considering that wide and often confusing and contradictory array of information, we must make judgments based upon data or surmise about patterns with which behaviors, or symptoms, have developed and coursed over the past, and how they may continue into the future. At the same time, one makes judgments about the particular value or relevance of certain classes of behaviors or aspects of style and, indeed, may decide not to change them even though they appear "symptomatic." It is quite possible that to do so could radically alter the psychological ecology of the individual and produce damaging consequences or, at the least, results of no merit.

Consequently, throughout the training enterprise supervisors, whether they be faculty, agency professionals supervising "clerkships," or internship supervisors, should keep in mind that the *primary* point of clinical training is not to provide exquisite skill in a particular procedure, but rather to develop the ability to make the best and most coherent judgments regarding prudent and effective treatment of a patient or group of patients. This requires a consistent and close supervisory relationship with a student, working, to the extent possible, on the development of single cases from inception to termination.

To develop this kind of decision-making approach to clinical training, it is important for students to have personal direct clinical experience, over time, with character disorders, neurotics, psychotics, and normals experiencing anxiety under stress. Further, it is imperative that students receive academic preparation and clinical training in representative approaches to assessment and treatment, ranging from projective to objective in the former case and from psychodynamic to behavioral in the latter. The importance of familiarity with clinical concepts and procedures, thorough knowledge of "basic" psychology, and the ability to enter the life space of patients in a fashion which permits the most effective "whole person" treatment decisions, cannot be overestimated.

FACILITIES

It appears obvious that it is unlikely, or impossible, that excellent clinical training can be provided when clinical experience is limited to one class of patients, to one physical location, or to one finite set of professionals. Clinical training, including experiences in psychotherapy, should be developed to meet the changing needs and interests of the student and should be altered over time. It is unlikely that quality clinical training at the pre-doctoral level can be accomplished in a tiny professional environment with limited professional input no matter how fine it might be. While it may not be possible for any individual student to take advantage of all training experiences potentially available, a broad range of opportunities should be developed, for example, work with severely disturbed patients, neurotics, children, adolescents and adults, normals under stress, outreach activities in community agencies, and applications of psychology to medicine and surgery. Thus, facilities for clinical training should extend beyond the university clinic which, as valuable as it may be, is perhaps too often considered the only resource "worthwhile" for students. While the clinical training offered in a "captive" environment may be excellent, it will nonetheless remain captive. Consequently, during the years at the university, students not only should be encouraged to seek regular and consistent supervision extending over time on individual cases in a number of agencies, but the training programs themselves should require such variety in training and in turn do everything possible to facilitate it, including the solicitation of well-selected internships away from campus if possible. If not possible, then these internships should at least provide significantly different or additional points of view.

STUDENT SELECTION, PROGRESS, AND COMPLETION/TERMINATION

I have heard it said that it is impossible to select good candidates for doctoral programs in clinical psychology without an opportunity for a detailed interview with them. I have also heard that it would be improper to select students with a total GRE score below ______ (you can fill in your own cutoff score here), and I have often heard students in Ph.D. programs described as inappropriate, not fit to continue, because they were too tense, too fat, laughed too much, were too quiet, (you can fill in the rest of this, too). If I had preconceptions about the kind of human raw material it takes to become an effective clinician, therapist, or academician, I have largely discarded them. Short of clearly demonstrable psychopathology, irretrievably bad judgment, or a motivational void, I doubt that any of us are able to identify characteristics which lead to failure or success.

Recently, I had an opportunity to learn of a former student of mine who left the graduate program after several years, under great fire from most faculty in the department. Although, as a matter of principle, I did not feel the student should have to leave, I eventually encouraged him to go because it was a practical matter, given the fact that attitudes of the faculty were so set against him. The student completed his Ph.D. at another clinical program and now, I have learned, has a very successful practice, and is highly regarded by clinical and academic peers in his community. I am sure most people who have been in clinical training settings over a period of time can recall similar stories. Probably many of them. For some reason, perhaps because we are clinicians, we may be so much aware of the "less than perfect" characteristics of our students that we tend to make dire predictions about how they will, after all, eventually turn out.

During my first clinical experience in a hospital, I marveled to my supervisor how many people actually were in such need of care that they were in the hospitals. He marveled back to me that, in turn, it was much more astounding to see how many people were not in the hospital and were quite able to get along, to lead reasonably happy and productive lives, and to find their way through life's tortuous pathways without ever seeking the help of a clinical psychologist or a psychiatrist. I remain much more impressed with the latter than with the former. However, the problem of selection remains a difficult one, and when decisions to terminate must be made on bases other than academic failure, as I believe they must on occasion, I confess to having no good ground rules or principles. Like all such matters, patience, kindness, and as much prudence as you can muster in the circumstances, should dictate the final choice. Not making the decision, or delaying it inordinately, may be the worst decision. However, I suggest the exercise of great caution in pursuing this course. If we as supervisors and evaluators are concerned about helping students and advancing the profession, we had best assiduously avoid acting, or believing that we are, psychologically sacrosanct and without emotional blemish, an obvious invocation to avoid the dynamisms of projection which are common in others.

PH.D. VERSUS PSY.D. VERSUS M.A.

In the 1960s, several forwardlooking programs began to develop graduate training programs leading to a terminal master's degree. That is, Ph.D.s, academicians, and practicing clinicians, began to realize that much of what was done in the practice of clinical psychology did not require either the highly selective initial filtering of candidates nor the level of training characteristic of Ph.D. programs. Much of assessment, patient management, and indeed treatment can be performed effectively by clinicians with less than the doctorate.

For a while, the notion gained momentum. It seems it gained momentum until the prospects of a large cadre of master's level psychologists in the clinical practice arena suggested the real possibility of an onerous group competing for limited resources. Another issue was the level of credentialing in relation to eligibility to receive third-party payments. Without being entirely crass about it, the direction was reversed. APA took the position that the proper educational level for practicing clinicians should be at the level of the doctorate, and generally showed conspicuously diminished interest in training at the master's level, although acknowledging that it still continued and probably would be so in the future.

After twenty years or so, the issue appears far from resolved. I believe that to be qualified as an independent practicing clinician, one should have a good foundation in psychology, a carefully designed professional curriculum, and an extensive amount of close, personal supervision on individual cases carefully followed over reasonable lengths of time, preferably six months to a year. It is not only important to learn the practices, it is also of paramount importance to learn the bases for making decisions which will lead to corrective experiences for patients. While I have strong reservations about how much such experience, as well as formal didactic training, can be received by a student in a conventional or near conventional master's program, I do believe that there is ample room in the profession for practice at the master's level or, as it is called in some states, the level of the examiner or technician.

At a broader level, however, we must continue to build a strong cadre of senior clinicians who have been reviewed by their peers and found worthy to carry the responsibility of the elder statesman supervisor, the clinical hallmark. To date, this has been best accomplished though the American Board of Professional Psychology (ABPP). Perhaps other devices will be developed whereby the profession will identify, in even better fashion, its senior members to occupy these clinical leadership positions. However, until that occurs, psychologists interested in pursuing independent clinical practice or clinical academic careers should pursue the Diplomate review procedures made available by ABPP.

On the other hand, the distinction between the Psy.D. and the Ph.D. does not appear terribly relevant in the evaluation and certification of clinical expertise. I have had the opportunity to visit a wide variety of Ph.D. clinical programs and several Psy.D. programs. I would not evaluate clinical students generally as superior or inferior in one or the other, although I have my own beliefs and prejudices about the quality of individual programs. The Psy.D. offers an opportunity to students, as have properly constructed Ph.D. programs, to gain education and clinical training sufficient to enter into post-doctoral experience which may lead them to the prospect of individual practice if they so choose. One of the most desirable aspects about opportunities for students to select Psy.D. or Ph.D. programs is that, at least in the case of the Psy.D., the intent of the program clearly is to produce clinical practitioners. When students have an opportunity to select from between the two, hopefully one would select the program offering educational experiences that would qualify one best for the professional activities anticipated.

Many, probably most, of our current Ph.D. programs still maintain a strong stated allegiance to preparing their students for research. And well they should. The Ph.D. is a research degree. However, the data show the overwhelming number of Ph.D. graduates in clinical psychology enter applied occupations and relatively few of them enter research and academic professions. Perhaps, as Psy.D. programs become better established and develop clearer identities, doctoral-level training in psychology may afford clearer distinctions between Psy.D. and Ph.D. programs and clearer opportunities for students to make informed choices among them. For the present, the nature of the Psy.D. and the programs for preparing Psy.D.s continue to emerge.

SUMMARY

The questions and comments presented in the preceding must appear to most readers to be covering old ground. Without doubt they appear that way to me. While I have no desire simply to make restatements, it does seem of considerable importance that so much of relevance to professional training in clinical psychology remains unsettled. It does not appear that we have established patterns of training insuring relatively comparable clinical experience at comparable levels of quality, that we hold common baseline expectations of faculty involved in clinical training, that the nature of patient populations and facilities required for training are identified, and so on. I do not suggest uniformity in these areas. Quite the opposite, university programs not only thrive on but also need the opportunity for diversity and individuality, in keeping with their own faculty and program objectives. On the other hand, it appears that there is a level of disarray that could have been dealt with better. Although the move toward certification of Departments of Psychology, the identification of health service providers, revisions in accreditation standards by APA, as well as ongoing discussions at the national level, address these issues, we do not seem yet to have gained on the problems appreciably. It is not the diversity itself which is of concern but rather the fact that students being educated and trained in our programs may, in addition to diversity, also show significant variations in levels of quality, no matter how considered. If that is so, it is incumbent upon us as ethical professionals to continue to address these issues, hopefully bring them into some reasonable balance and harmony, and assure to the extent possible the qualifications of our graduates.

The Future of Clinical Training in Psychotherapy

Ronald B. Kurz

Training in psychotherapy in the future will be affected, as it has been in the past, by the recent developments and the fads and fancies of our field. In the 1960s and 1970s, various forms of behavior therapy and behavior modification rose in prominence and were seen as the wave of the future. In the 1970s and early 1980s, family therapy in its several forms seems to be taking hold. Also for the 1980s, the melding of medical and psychological concerns in assessment and treatment, as seen in such fields as health psychology, pediatric psychology, and behavioral medicine, will probably continue to have an increasingly strong effect on how therapists approach their patients. As the new approaches develop and their efficacy begins to be tested, they influence the content of therapeutic training. The influence appears to be additive. Older therapeutic approaches appear not to be dropped from training programs; rather they must compete, often very successfully, with the newer forms. For example, in an analysis of psychology internship training program characteristics (Kurz, 1982), it was found that the predominant theoretical orientation of internship program staffs was psychodynamic, although most training programs described themselves as eclectic. It appears that the older psychoanalytically-oriented approaches continue to be taught along with the more recently developed forms of treatment.

Whereas developments in the theory and data of the field affect the content of psychotherapy training, they have little apparent effect on the process of training, on who does the training, or on who the trainees will be. The latter issues will be the focus of this chapter. I will suggest that there are currently social and economic forces at work that will change the way we train therapists, whom we will select for training, and who does the training. These same social and economic forces will undoubtedly influence the content of training as well, but the attention in this chapter will be on the process matters.

Social forces affecting the process of training is not a recent phenomenon. One need only look back over the last twenty years at the social upheaval of the 1960s and early 1970s to see profound social and economic effects. Two important examples can be noted. One is the community mental health movement, with its concern for getting patients out of hospitals and treating them in the community. The other is the civil rights movement which opened education and job opportunities in the professions to members of minority groups and to women. Both had profound effects on clinical training in the mental health fields. In the first example, practicum, field training, and internship training were opened up to include community settings, paraprofessionals, and an emphasis on community action, consultation and prevention, rather than on one-to-one treatment. It is not incidental that the 1965 Chicago Conference on clinical psychology training (Hoch, Ross, & Winder, 1966) recommended that university training programs include community-based trainers in their programs, and that the programs responded by increasing their appointments of such persons (Simmons, 1971). In the second example, professional training programs in the mental health fields responded in varying degrees to the civil rights issues of the time by increasing minority and women enrollments, and recruiting minority and women faculty, which in turn fostered the development of additional training in the special mental health needs of minority persons and women (Schneider, 1981).

Furrow (1983) identifies four factors that are likely to transform the practice of psychotherapy in the 1980s. Writing from an attorney's perspective, he cites fear of malpractice suits, research into biological factors in mental illness, third-party financing of treatment, and the increasing practice of psychotherapy within corporate medicine, as prominent influences. Anxiety about malpractice suits over iatrogenic harm to patients is increasing and may end up cluttering the minds of therapists with the trauma of litigation. Although the reality is that suits are rarely brought, therapists are becoming increasingly anxious because of the spectacular publicity and notoriety over the few cases involving the failure to warn others regarding the dangerousness of their patients, as well as cases of therapists having sex with patients. Nevertheless, the number of malpractice suits against therapists is rising (Roth & Levin, 1983; Taub, 1983), and with it there has been a rise in therapists' anxiety. Such anxiety about malpractice affects not only the practice of psychotherapy but the teaching of it as well. In such an environment, training may be expected to become more conservative. Trainees will be encouraged to stick to what can be demonstrated to be effective; and since in most states the licensed supervisors are liable for errors of their unlicensed supervisees, there may be greater attention paid to training activities. Supervisors may become more careful, not only with listening to, observing, and teaching their students, but also with increased interest in the selection of therapeutic techniques, the selection of clients their students treat, and the selection of the trainees themselves. In an era of proliferation of therapeutic approaches, there are many who will welcome a consolidation to a (hopefully) few that work and a more responsible attitude toward trainees.

As research on the organic factors in mental illness and the biological treatments of them accelerate, there will be increasing demands for parallel studies of the psychological mechanisms of verbal forms of psychotherapy and a demonstration of their efficacy. Furrow (1983) suggests that therapists who continue to use verbal forms of treatment in the face of evidence of demonstrated effectiveness of biological treatments may be liable for the client's slow progress or deterioration. Thus, this biological trend is yet another area that brings threats of malpractice suits and, with it, greater conservatism in our selection of treatments, trainees, and clients. Furthermore, the biological hypothesis may become so compelling that it could shake the very core of traditional verbal psychotherapy, including the research hypotheses and methodologies we choose (American Psychiatric Association, 1982). Such a revolution would have profound effects on the kind of trainees who enter the psychotherapy profession and on their attitudes toward being trained in purely psychological modes of treatment. For example, Klein et al. (1980) discuss anxiety, a central issue in most forms of traditional verbal psychotherapy, as a biological event, rather than an interpersonal or psychosocial one. If such a hypothesis and its consequent treatments are found to be efficacious, who will be attracted to verbal and humanistically-oriented treatments? Psychotherapy training may well be left to the nonmedical fields of psychology and social work, but here as well, the biological shadow will be felt. Already we find accommodations to it as training increasingly involves the "biopsychosocial" approach (Engel, 1977). Future training of psychotherapists may therefore involve greater emphasis on the biological bases of behavior, with greater interface between psychosocial therapists and medical personnel. This shift will likely bring about training programs which will foster the mixing of traditional verbally-oriented clinicians with trainees and faculty members from primarily basic, nontherapy disciplines such as a biopsychology, physiological psychology, neuropsychology, and pharmacology.

Expanded third-party financing of psychotherapy is another major force converging on the practice of psychotherapy. The promise of insurance reimbursement has brought increasing competition to the mental health arena and pressure to use methods that are demonstrably effective. In their efforts to cut costs, third-party payers will demand justification for the often less efficient verbal psychotherapies. Third-party reimbursement is already creating problems for the training of psychotherapists in some fields, and this area of confusion is likely to be with us for a while. In some jurisdictions, insurance companies will only pay if a licensed practitioner actually sees the client. Training programs have devised ways around this problem. For example, the obvious approach is to have unlicensed trainees treat only self-pay or charity clients. Another is to have student therapists in co-therapy collaborations with their licensed supervisors. In any event, training programs will find it increasingly difficult to train therapists in traditional ways with traditional clients. Self-pay and charity clients may represent a skewed population, with different sets of problems, dynamics and expectancies, calling for different therapeutic approaches, when compared with insured clients. Direct observation and co-therapy may be appropriate with group therapy and family treatment, but they are usually considered unacceptable in the traditional forms of individual psychotherapy.

Private corporations are expanding into medical practices, including the purchase of psychiatric hospitals, substance abuse centers, and behavioral medicine enterprises (Starr, 1982). The purchase of training hospitals is apparently not exempt from corporate control. Private, for-profit treatment of the mentally ill is likely to triple by the end of this decade (A New Market, 1982). An emphasis on short-term treatment, more therapists working in group settings than in private practice, and greater concern for malpractice issues will be likely results of the move to corporate control (Furrow, 1982). Since the corporation will be liable for its therapists' actions, with obvious earnings implications, it will tighten control over what its therapists do. Psychotherapy trainees may not be welcome in such an environment. Trainees are costly, they may be less efficient than fully-trained professionals, and they are perhaps more likely to make mistakes leading to the threat of malpractice suits. Clients may be more willing to sue when the therapist-client relationship is imbedded within a corporate structure (Furrow, 1983). When training programs become part of profit-making enterprises, the onus will be on the program to demonstrate to the corporate managers that trainees are cost-effective, and to accrediting and credentialing bodies that the educational integrity of the programs is preserved and that the trainees are not being exploited for the profit of the corporation.

Until the mid-1970s, economic and political conditions favored the growth of mental health training programs. Federal money, largely in the form of training grants from the National Institute of Mental Health and training stipends from the Veterans Administration, flowed freely to students interested in careers involving psychotherapy. The funds had a significant and well-documented influence on the development of the mental health fields (Kirsch & Winter, 1983; Schneider, 1981) in general, and on psychotherapy training in particular. Large numbers of trainees who could not otherwise afford to obtain graduate education and training in psychotherapy were enabled to do so by these grants and stipends. NIMH funds have been particularly helpful in the recruitment and retention of minority trainees (Schneider, 1981). Starting in the 1970s, and accelerating in the 1980s, there has been a serious reduction in financial aid available to trainees, the consequences of which are just beginning to be felt. Not only is tuition and other financial support drying up, but this has been happening in a period of strong inflationary pressures on tuition and other living expenses. The likely result is that the mental health fields will only be able to attract an elite of wealthy students who can afford to pay their own way. In an area where cultural and ethnic diversity of practitioners is seen as a necessity (American Psychological Association, 1979), we are now faced with an insufficient pool of ethnically and culturally diverse trainees. Training programs will need to make special efforts to ensure training in cultural diversity. Since the minority and lower-SES students in training programs have themselves been an important source of pressure on programs to provide the appropriate training experiences, the trainers will have an increased responsibility to maintain appropriate breadth in the programs.

A related issue is that the mental health fields are attracting increasingly large numbers of women. The same social forces that mandated greater opportunities for minority students and for broadening the cultural diversity of training programs, also mandated the opening of the fields to women. Whereas only modest success was achieved with minority enrollments, which is now being threatened by the cut-back in training grants and stipends, training programs are now beginning to report that the majority of their applicants are women and that they could quickly become trainers of primarily women therapists (American Psychological Association, 1983). The reasons for this development can only be surmised at this time, but it is believed to be economic. Salaries in the psychotherapy fields have not kept up with those in careers in other areas of science and business. Men are being drawn away from work as psychotherapists, leaving the field to women. For whatever reason, if this trend continues it will have a profound effect on training. One result is that the economic disadvantage of the field will accelerate, and even less money will be available for training. Another very different result will be increasing demands for training in feminist therapies and a focus on neglected issues of gender-related problems. At the same time, the women trainees will find themselves in training programs which, for a while at least, will remain dominated by male faculties and staff. The search for female clinical role models and the potential for male-female culture conflict in training programs could intensify.

Economic factors have brought us to the limits of growth in new training programs for psychotherapists. Indeed, as the effects of the great cuts in NIMH funding ripples through the traditional university programs, there may well be a noticeable reduction in the size of clinical training facilities. There is no sign yet, however, that the demand for training in the psychotherapy fields is diminishing. Traditional programs may be tempted to maintain the sizes of their classes to bring in tuitions and to justify their training roles. Furthermore, free-standing professional schools, which are heavily dependent on tuition, whether profit-making or non-profit, may expand as they take up the students turned away from the shrinking traditional university programs. In either case, as the ties to traditional training values of small classes and individual attention and supervision are weakened, accreditation and credentialing issues will assume even more importance than they carry now. Psychotherapy training programs will have to monitor their adherence to academic standards with great care in order to maintain accreditation and to assure their students that they will be eligible for licensure and board certification.

An important outcome of the expected lack of growth in new training programs and the possible contraction of old ones is that the faculties and training staffs will be aging and heavily tenured. The usual influx of new, untenured faculty members who bring cross-fertilization and stimulation, will slow to a trickle. The implications of this will be several. First, training for therapists could be in danger of stultifying unless faculties find ways of including newly trained therapists of various persuasions as trainers in their programs. Second, there may be greater potential for culture clash between young trainees and their older supervisors. Third, there may develop a greater interest in training therapists to treat a maturing and aging population. This latter interest may develop both from the increasing number of aged persons in the population at large and from the interests and concerns of the maturing faculties.

In this chapter, I have tried to predict how several social and economic factors that are currently impinging on psychotherapy training will affect training in the near future. The last decade has seen a tremendous growth in the concern for credentialing in the mental health fields (Sales, 1983). As I have indicated in several instances above, pressure for standards and credentials will probably continue to increase. Despite the negative outcome I have suggested from some of the forces I have described, our continuing interest in standards for ourselves and for our trainees will have a corrective effect on the direction of training activities. It would be easy, for example, to expand programs, to seek profits from the labors of our trainees, to train only in the most efficient forms of treatment without regard to other humanistic values, and to overlook the importance of ethnic and cultural diversity in training psychotherapists. I do not think we will allow ourselves to take the easy paths.

REFERENCES

A New Market for Hospital Chains. *Business Week*, 1983, April 11, p. 12.

American Psychiatric Association. *Psychotherapy research: Methodological and efficacy issues.* Washington, D.C.: Author, 1982.

American Psychological Association. *Criteria for accreditation of doctoral training programs and internships in professional psychology.* Washington, D.C.: Author, 1979.

American Psychological Association. *Conference of Psychology Training Program Directors.* Washington, D.C.: 1983.

Cowen, E.L. Community mental health and primary prevention. In I.B. Weiner (Ed.), *Clinical methods in psychology,* 2nd. Ed. New York: Wiley, 1983, pp. 634-694.

Engel, G.L. The need for a new medical model: A challenge for biomedicine. *Science,* 1977, *196,* 129-136.

Furrow, B.R. Will psychotherapy be transformed in the 1980s? *Law, Medicine and Health Care,* 1983, *11,* 96-117.

Hoch, E.L., Ross, A.O. & Winder, C.L. *Professional preparation of clinical psychologists.* Washington, D.C.: American Psychological Association, 1965.

Kirsch, K. & Winter, C. A history of clinical psychology. In C.E. Walker (Ed.), *The handbook of clinical psychology.* Homewood, Illinois: Dow-Jones Irwin, 1983, pp. 3-30.

Klein, D.F., Gittleman, R., Quitkin, F. & Rifkin, A. *Diagnosis and drug treatment of psychiatric disorders: Adults and children.* 2nd Ed. Baltimore: William and Wilkins, 1980, pp. 493-507.

Kurz, R.B., Fuchs, M., Dabek, R.F., Kurtz, S.M.S. & Helfrich, W.T. Characteristics of predoctoral internships in professional psychology. *American Psychologist,* 1982, *37,* 1213-1220.

Roth, M.D. & Levin, L.J. Dilemma of Tarasoff: Must physicians protect the public or their patients? *Law, Medicine and Health Care,* 1983, *11,* 104-131.

Sales, B.D. (Ed.) *The professional psychologist's handbook.* New York: Plenum, 1983.

Schneider, S.F. Where have all the students gone: Position of psychologists trained in clinical/services programs. *American Psychologist,* 1981, *36,* 1427-1449.

Simmons, W.L. Clinical training programs, 1964-1965 and 1968-1969: A characterization and comparison. *American Psychologist,* 1971, *26,* 717-721.

Starr, P. *The social transformation of American Medicine.* New York: Basic Books, 1982.

Taub, S. *Psychiatric malpractice in the 1980s:* A look at some areas of concern. *Law, Medicine and Health Care,* 1983, *11,* 97-135.

CONCLUSION

Afterwisdom

Tom H. Peake
Robert P. Archer

> The art of progress is to preserve order amid change and to preserve change amid order.
>
> —Alfred North Whitehead

The impetus for this volume came from the first editor's frustration and enjoyment in developing internship training programs over the last 10 years. It gained momentum as the coeditors worked together in training psychotherapy students and subtly retraining some supervisors as well (ourselves included). Spurred by insights and problems that have arisen in supervision and in seminars on "The Process of Supervision," we wanted to invite several authors (included here) who had influenced our own thinking and growth to help us produce a developmental map for the best psychotherapy training. We thought we knew what we would produce as we invited our friends and mentors to contribute. In some ways we have been surprised by the results.

We hoped for a monolithic developmental map. None emerged. What did emerge were several developmental maps, a confirmation of our hunch that much psychotherapy training is influenced by inadvertent factors, and an expectation that training and supervision can be improved by using the wisdom of several developmental schemes.

The clinician should emerge from training with a professional identity that includes a realistic sense of mastery, and a realistic sense of limitations, while retaining the idealism that fuels continued growth. That is the best development.

It is absurd to expect that a book of readings will guarantee good training, but it can preview and review the *contexts* of learning. If we properly anticipate nuances of new experiences and donate *after-wisdom* about the meaning of enigmatic past experiences, we learn better.

William James reportedly said that we learn to swim in the winter and to ice skate in the summer. Any student of psychotherapeutics has memories of being stressed, overimmersed, or plainly baffled by certain aspects of his or her training. James seems to be talking about the wonderful consolidation and resolve of understanding which appears long after that particularly difficult client has us tied in (a) excruciating knots of transference and counter transference, (b) matrices of contradictory reinforcement contingencies, or (c) a double-bind without the aid of subtitles.

At this point the value of "horror stories" is worth mentioning. Interns or residents who have extended contact with each other invariably spend some informal time in the ritual of exchanging horror stories about their most awful experiences. This may be about a professor, a patient, a clinic or placement where they worked, or some ghastly treatment error. The ritual is similar to veterans' exchanging war stories. In some ways a compendium of horror stories, factor analyzed, edited and indexed would be a priceless concordance for the training journey (perhaps a sequel?). Short of that, horror stories are still valuable. Exchanging training trauma tales promotes commonality between the tellers, helps reduce cognitive dissonance that the training effort is worthwhile even though it is emotionally costly, and serves a warning or survival function which might be called antimodeling, or what not to do. Finally, by contrast, the horror stories elevate the value of those positive experiences which build confidence and mastery. This dimension of *afterwisdom* describes the process of learning to swim in the winter.

The *contexts* of learning, mentioned earlier, is an important concept for training. These readings should be useful in cueing contexts of training and simply enhancing our sensitivity to the contexts of learning. In his essay on "The Logical Categories of Learning and Communication," Gregory Bateson (1972) distinguishes among several types of learning. His distinction between Learning I and Learning II is the most pertinent, because it helps in doing psychotherapy and in learning how to do psychotherapy. The learning principles apply to client and clinician alike. Learning I includes (a) rote learning where some behavior becomes a stimulus for another behavior, (b) "completed" learning that is changed by disruption, extinction, or inhibition, (c) habituation to not respond where the individual once did, and (d) conditioning of either respondent or operant types. This learning is described as a *change in specificity of response* by correcting errors of choice from a set of alternatives. In contrast, Learning II is a *change in the process of Learning I* where other sets of alternatives are used to correct the choice. This entails "a change in how the sequence of experience is punctuated," (Bateson, 1972, p. 293). This type of learning is also referred to as learning to learn, transfer of learning, or deuterolearning. Learning II is qualitatively different from Learning I. The higher form learning requires a sensitivity to the contexts that tell when a set of alternatives is inappropriate and when other sets are needed. When a client accomplishes this shift (Peake et al., 1979) from one perspective or mode of approach to a problem to a more useful perspective, it is called "*insight.*" The psychodynamic concept of transference insight is a special example. When a trainee uses Learning II, he or she both develops alternative sets of perspectives for dealing with problems as well as sensitively considers the contextual cues that suggest the correct set. Training must address both learning to read contextual cues and developing a repertoire of context sets or problem-solving perspectives.

A similar contextual shift has been described by Piaget in a deceptively simple way. Piaget's prototype description of a child's cognitive growth reveals much about continued adult cognitive growth. Borrowing the concepts of *equilibration, assimilation, accommodation,* and *schema* from Piaget, Ginsburg and Opper (1969) consider their application to training. *Schema* is a cognitive representation of some set of operations or relationships, i.e., a thought structure or framework. In assimilation an individual organizes and incorporates facts, information, and abstractions into existing schemata. When a child's cognitive growth occurs, the move from one stage to the next produces a qualitative change marked by alteration of existing schemata. *Accommodation* is this upheaval or cognitive shift where the prior cognitive structures are no longer adequate to incorporate or assimilate the experience(s) or data. New schemata or cognitive frameworks must be developed, and assimilation begins again at the new stage. Cognitive growth with a qualitatively new perspective has occurred. The interaction of these complementary processes of assimilation and accommodation is called *equilibration.* The same processes that describe children's cognitive growth can also describe adult cognitive growth. A goal of psychotherapy training likewise should be continued contextual learning and ongoing equilibration of this unique, emotion-laden knowledge.

An example of this in a clinician's development would be the shift from the self, viewed as student, to the self, viewed as practicing professional. This shift implies a good deal of contextual learning, accommodation and then assimilation. It is an emotional as well as intellectual growth. A good training combines challenging experiences which force reconsideration of schemata and opportunities to reunderstand (i.e., accommodate then reassimilate) under the tutelage of mature mentors.

Another issue, creative process in clinical skills, bears mention. Rollo May (1975) has given a discerning account of the elements of form and passion that must be balanced in creative endeavors, including human relationships. May (1975) suggests that "consciousness is the awareness that emerges out of the dialectical tension between possibilities and limitations" (p. 114). Realizing limits of the human personality can be expanding in that a sense of personal responsibility, a loneliness, and therefore a sense of the need for love, becomes clearer. In this respect, limiting and expanding go together. Producing a poem requires fitting emotion into a certain form. Fitting an understandable form requires searching the imagination. That can produce new meanings. Psychotherapy is also a curious mixture of form and emotion. A therapist's passion for providing an insight must be channeled into an understandable form or it is purposeless. A patient's overwhelming feeling needs an acceptable structure of expression. As imagination gives life to form, structure or form keeps imagination (or passion) channeled and therefore useful.

The artistry and emotion of psychotherapy must be tempered by the form, ethics, empiricism, and method that science provides. The entire process is also tempered by societal and economic factors. In that respect, another kind of equilibration is seen to be important for the clinician. An ongoing balancing and rebalancing of form and passion is the structure for a therapist's growth.

As the quote that began this final chapter reflects, progress is the art of producing a correct balance of order amid change and change amid order. Piaget, Bateson, and May's models are additional ways of conceiving this balance, along with the other developmental models and maps our authors have given. We have discovered that training in psychotherapy develops: (a) in the individual student, (b) in the supervisory dyad, and (c) in the organizational and economic contexts of our society. A unitary developmental scheme cannot cover all those dimensions, but the equilibration of change and order will help us best continue to improve psychotherapy training.

REFERENCES

Bateson, G. *Steps to an ecology of mind.* New York: Ballantine Books, 1972.

Ginsburg, H., & Opper, S. *Piaget's theory of intellectual development.* Englewood Cliffs, New Jersey: Prentice-Hall, 1969.

May, R. *The courage to create.* New York: Norton., 1975.

Peake, T., Van Noord, R., & Albott, W. Psychotherapy as an altered state of awareness. *Journal of Contemporary Psychotherapy,* 1979, *10,* 98-104.